LIVING

NEPHESH

BECOMING WHOLE IN
BREATH AND BODY

LIVING

NEPHESH

PAYTON B. FOUST MD

Published by Living Nephesh Media, Lexington, South Carolina

ISBN 979-8-9993099-0-7, Hardcover

ISBN 979-8-9993099-1-4, Paperback

ISBN 979-8-9993099-2-1, eBook

Book designed by Mark Karis.

Published in the United States of America.

CONTENTS

AUTHOR'S NOTE

WRITING THIS BOOK CHANGED MY LIFE.

Not just because I was moved by its convictions.

Not just because in writing it I experienced something singular—receiving, rather than striving to produce.

Not just because I learned the quiet fruits of obedience, answering a call I never expected: an utter nonauthor called to authorship.

But because it pointed me back to God's goodness.

And that goodness has met me not only in my own life but in the stories of those I've cared for—their struggles, their resilience, their questions, and their hope. It is through their journeys that this book truly took shape.

Every clinical vignette in this book is rooted in a real person. A few details have been changed to protect privacy, but the soul of each story remains.

As I reflected on each chapter's truth, I remembered these living souls with God-given clarity:

The challenges.

The frustrations.

The hurt.

The change.

The healing.

The victories—some seismic, some no bigger than a sigh of relief.

Looking back on these ten years of practice in this place I call home, I was overcome with gratitude.

A gratitude that brought wholeness.

A gratitude that gave breath to this vision.

A gratitude that reminded me—again—that even the wounded can become vessels of healing.

Even the weary can become whole.

And to every soul who has entrusted their care to me—thank you.

I have entrusted you to the Father.

And He has met me again and again in the sacred spaces we've shared—in this messy, visceral, beautiful thing we call the practice of medicine.

Dear reader, this book is for you too—

For the ones whose souls have grown tired but not extinguished.

For those still breathing, still hoping, still aching for wholeness.

You are not forgotten.

You are not alone.

And you, too, are a living *nephesh*:

A carrier of breath.

A witness to restoration still unfolding.

INTRODUCTION

MY STORY, like yours, begins with a longing for something more—a desire for a life that's whole. That longing eventually led me home—to a life of medicine, faith, and rediscovery.

I'm a family physician—board certified, practicing in a rural community less than two minutes from the home where I grew up. Many would caution against returning to your hometown to practice medicine, warning of the challenges that come with blurring personal and professional lines in a small town. But returning home taught me more than medicine ever could. It taught me who God is—and it revealed the way into which Jesus calls us.

When I entered medical school, I thought I had a clear vision for the kind of physician God was calling me to become: a surgical specialist, likely trained at a prestigious academic center in a major city. But as I rotated through each specialty—surgery, radiology, obstetrics—I appreciated aspects of them all, yet none felt like home. That changed at the end of my first clinical year, when I returned to my hometown for a family medicine rotation at a Federally Qualified Health Center. By the end I recognized a calling I couldn't ignore: to return home and practice primary care.

Coming out of a training environment in medical school that often felt more secular than sacred—where an attending once referred to *The God Delusion* during our graduation as required reading—I found unexpected grace. I matched, by God's providence, at a rural residency program that combined robust clinical training with a strong faith-based mission, serving both local and international communities. It was there I realized that medicine—particularly family medicine—is more than a profession. It is, in many ways, a ministry. While we doctors tend to bodies and pastors tend to souls, the lines between the two blur beautifully—especially when we invite them to.

Over the past decade of practice, I've discovered a few disheartening tensions. First, pathology can't be explained through simple, reductionist categories. Take depression: It's rarely just physical, neurochemical, relational, or spiritual—it's often all of the above, indivisibly. Genuine healing, or what we call *remission* in medicine, comes only through a truly holistic approach, addressing both body and soul.

Second, the way healthcare is often delivered can leave people feeling more fragmented than whole. The more "-ologists" I see in a patient's chart, the deeper the division seems to grow within them.

Third, we—myself included—are searching for wholeness in a world bent on pulling us apart. I've watched people try to fill that void through religion or pleasure, monogamy or indulgence, rigorous discipline or unchecked consumption. But the question always remains: What is the missing piece within me, and how do I find it?

Through countless patient encounters, God has graciously guided me back not to a simple solution but to the beginning. The very beginning. Genesis 2.

I've come to see that God is calling us back to reclaim a vision as old as Eden.

We often focus on the fall in Genesis 3 as the tragic rupture between Adam and God—which it was. But we may miss what happened within Adam himself. His soul—his *nephesh*—fractured from his body. The living nephesh God had created, fully integrated and unified, suffered disintegration. We feel that ache in every part of life: in our mental health, physical health, relationships, and restless search for meaning.

In a world where knowledge of the body expands exponentially, where healthcare systems grow ever more complex and yet outcomes often disappoint, there is still hope. God beckons us back to Edenic wholeness. Through Jesus, we are invited home—into a life where body and spirit are no longer in conflict but in communion with the Breath-Giver.

This book isn't about quick fixes or religious platitudes. It's about finding our way back to the integrated, embodied life God intended—a life of breath, body, belonging, becoming, and blessing. An invitation to live nephesh. To restore the dust of our bodies back to the Breath that gives life.

THE JOURNEY UNFOLDS IN THREE MOVEMENTS

Part 1 explores what was lost in the garden: how Adam and Eve experienced disintegration, the frameworks we've inherited to heal that wound, and the true healing that comes through the way of Jesus.

Part 2 considers how we begin to live whole again: how the Spirit invites us to name our fractures, take grace-filled steps toward healing, and build a sustainable rule of life that helps us abide as nephesh in the Vine.

Part 3 explores wholeness in everyday life: where formation meets fatigue, vocation meets vulnerability, and healing is ongoing.

This book is for anyone seeking wholeness. You don't need theological training or medical knowledge to engage. Whether you're a skeptic, a believer, a healthcare worker, or simply someone longing for a more integrated life—you're welcome here. My sincerest hope is that this book will meet you where you are and offer a vision of wholeness worth living.

Thank you for trusting me with your attention—and with your story.

Then the L*ORD* *God formed a man from the dust of the ground and breathed into his nostrils the breath of life, and the man became a living being [nephesh].*

GENESIS 2:7

The glory of God is a human being fully alive.

IRENAEUS

PART I

THE VISION: WHAT WE LOST

1

BREATH AND DUST

Then the LORD God formed a man from the dust of the ground and breathed into his nostrils the breath of life, and the man became a living being.

GENESIS 2:7

BREATH IN, BREATH OUT.

For all eternity, unbound by time and space, God has breathed in perfect cadence.

In a dance of endless giving and receiving, the Father, Son, and Holy Spirit moved in perfect unity—overflowing in love, complete in belonging.

The Breath-Giver needed nothing.

Yet from the fullness of His life, He breathed outward—and the dust stirred.

It was not necessity that shaped the world but joy.

Not loneliness but love.

Not obligation but overflow.

And in the quiet of that overflow, the Creator gathered dust in His hands. He bent low, drawing impossibly near, molding what no other creature in heaven or earth could claim: a being of dust and spirit, earthly and divine, animated by His own breath—His *ruach*.

This is where the story of humanity begins—in wholeness, not in brokenness. Before shame, before strife, before the fracture between spirit and flesh, there was only union. This was all the universe had ever known. The first human did not awaken as a divided being, torn in tension between body and soul. He was a living soul—*nephesh*, in Hebrew—a whole person, alive in every sense, fully at peace. He walked not only in the presence of God but in rhythm within himself. Breath and body, dust and spirit, life and belonging—all one.

That same cosmic dance enjoyed for all eternity within the triune Creator had been breathed into man.

PERFECT HARMONY WITHIN

Eden granted humanity a priceless gift: unbroken fellowship with God. Scripture portrays this vividly, with Adam walking alongside the Creator in the cool of the day. In this simple image, we see Adam experience integration. Walking with God was not simply spiritual, nor was it simply physical: It was indivisibly both. He enjoyed unblemished communion with his Father, wholly loved. What God enjoyed in Trinity for all eternity, He shared with His created son.

But even in Eden, God recognized that it was not good for man to be alone. The same voice that had spoken perfection, completion, and goodness over all creation declared that wholeness was never meant to be enjoyed alone.

From Adam's side came Eve.

In her, Adam recognized another body, another soul—a nephesh like his own. Bone of his bone, flesh of his flesh, animated by God's same breath.

Together they reflected the rhythm of the Trinity: distinct, united, whole.

Their lives unfolded in seamless rhythm. They named and nurtured side by side, shoulder to shoulder, their heartbeats rhyming with each other's and with that of their Father's. In each other they found echo and expression—at their very core, the same breath, the same belonging, the same resonance. They stood before each other unashamed, each a living reflection of God's provision and intimate care.

Work, worship, relationship—even the simple act of eating—in the garden were all expressions of integrated living. Every heartbeat, every breath, every step was worship. Perfectly aligned with their Father, they knew no need. No shame, no nakedness, no isolation or abandonment. They were fully themselves, fully human, fully present. They lived in embodied certainty that they were created to be loved by God and to walk in relationship with Him.

God established clear rhythms of life for them. With His breath, He instilled in them the same creative power and ambition with which He had created the entire cosmos. Their bodies, molded from the dust laid upon God's created masterpiece, had been formed by the very hands of the Maker. They wielded their bodies as an act of worship, a remembrance of God's intentional and complete design. They used them to work, to shepherd, and to cultivate God's creation. Though naked, they moved throughout the created order unashamed, walking boldly in step with and in the presence of the Father.

Belonging was instinct.

Without striving, without fracture, in wholeness they grew, flourished, became who God created them to be.

Their days unfolded like breath—work and rest, tending and delight, seamlessly woven into one rhythm of being. There were no divided selves, no compartments to manage, no distinction between sacred and ordinary. The garden didn't demand balance; it offered harmony. Even rest was not recovery. It was communion—a return not from depletion but to goodness.

This was what it meant to live as nephesh: living souls, whole and unhurried.

Yet even in Eden, wholeness was not beyond disruption.

It wasn't Adam and Eve's striving that sustained integration, but alignment—their breath, their being, their instincts attuned to the rhythm of their Creator. This was entrusted, not earned. Received, not manufactured. Still, it was vulnerable.

The soil of Eden was sacred, yes—but not untouchable.

Even paradise had a gate.

If you lean in close, you can almost hear it:

A whisper beneath the rustling leaves.

A breath hesitating in the stillness.

For even in perfection, there was space for choice.

For listening. For turning.

It is easy to think of Eden as a place long lost, its gates sealed behind us. But perhaps Eden is not so much a place as it is a posture—a way of being. A way of breathing. A way of remembering that wholeness was our beginning. That we were not made to be fragmented, hurried, or isolated but to live integrated in the rhythm of God's own breath.

That rhythm calls to us still.

Even now when our days feel scattered and our bodies tired, the invitation lingers like a fragrance on the air. It is not a call to recreate Eden by our own efforts.

It is a call to return to the breath that made us.

To remember that before anything broke, we were made whole.

Pause here.

Take a few moments to breathe slowly—in and out.

Let your breath anchor you in the truth: You were not made to be divided, rushed, or fractured.

As you breathe, let its cadence restore you to the sacred rhythm of your Creator.

Imagine walking with Him in the cool of the day—fully seen, fully known.

You were formed from dust but animated by divine breath.

You were made not to be managed in parts but lived as a whole.

REFLECTION: REMEMBERING WHOLENESS

- Where do you feel most at home in your own body and spirit right now, fully integrated?

- Where do you feel most fragmented?

- What does it stir in you to imagine that before anything broke, you were created for harmony—with God, with yourself, and with others?

LET THIS REMEMBERING BE YOUR FIRST STEP—

NOT TOWARD FIXING BUT TOWARD RETURNING.

2

THE FRACTURE

And they heard the sound of the LORD God walking in the garden in the cool of the day, and the man and his wife hid themselves from the presence of the LORD God among the trees of the garden. But the LORD God called to the man and said to him, "Where are you?"

GENESIS 3:8-9

SHE SAT ACROSS FROM ME, in the office for routine follow up, just as she had many times before. Thirty-six years old. A mother, a wife, a believer. As I asked how she was doing, her eyes searched the corners of the room, welling up with tears. Taking a few tissues from the box, she explained that she had spent the past decade trying to will herself into wholeness. She had lost—and found again—the same twenty pounds twice this year already. She had tried to live an integrated life—Whole30, Mediterranean diet, tithed faithfully, exercised consistently.

But she still felt divided.

"I just ... can't seem to get it all to fall into place at the same time. When I'm consistent with my diet, I lose momentum with my morning

Bible study. When I'm faithful in prayer and quiet time, my body feels like it's falling apart. I feel like I'm living in pieces."

This is a story I encounter with heartbreaking frequency.

A modern expression of an ancient problem.

A new shape to an old wound.

With the fall, the intimacy, the comfort, the wholeness that came from perfect communion with the Father was disrupted. Sin introduced guilt. And with it, a new kind of awareness—no longer rooted in belovedness but in exposure. A consciousness marked by nakedness, isolation, and separation. Adam and Eve's walks with their Creator were replaced by a new instinct: hiding. Relational rupture gave way to displacement. Out of the garden. Out of communion. Out of rhythm with the created order.

But the fracture didn't stop at the boundary of the garden.

It took root within them.

Once whole and in lockstep with the very breath that animated them, humanity now lived with an internal shattering. The nephesh—that unity of body and spirit, once fully integrated and indivisible—sheared apart. Their bodies, formed in God's image, still bore His breath. But now they carried the weight of shame, toil, and decay. Their souls ached for God with a hunger they had never known. Yet that ache, rather than drawing them homeward, often sent them searching elsewhere—a disoriented hunger, marked by confusion, fear, and grasping.

This is the fracture that echoes in us still. We feel it in our restlessness, in our striving, in our chronic sense that something deep, something profound is lacking. Modern language may name it *stress, dysregulation, burnout*. Scripture names it *exile*. And it is not only physical separation from Eden. It is a soul still aching for home.

The psalmist, with pained refrain, gives voice to this longing: "Why, my [nephesh], are you downcast? Why so disturbed within me?" (Psalm 42:5). His exquisite clarity and honest lament reveal both the disorientation and disintegration of the fracture. Like so many before and after him, he names what Pascal would later call the "infinite abyss" (often referred to as a "God-shaped hole")[1]—recognizing the disturbance of the soul but not its remedy. The symptom but not yet the cure.

This disintegration is not limited to an unlucky few. Paul bears witness to it in Romans 8:22: "We know that the whole creation has been groaning as in the pains of childbirth right up to the present time." The schism of the living soul is profound: visceral, spiritual, universal.

Made in the image of their triune Father, humanity suffered the pain of this divorce both inwardly and outwardly. Cain takes Abel's life. Adam blames Eve—the very flesh of his flesh—for his disobedience. James names the dynamic in his epistle: "What causes quarrels and what causes fights among you? Is it not this, that your passions are at war within you?" (James 4:1 ESV). The echoes of triune wholeness once shared in the garden between Adam and Eve are now painfully on display through their disintegration—what was once mutual delight now marked by distance, distrust, and rivalry.

Even now, millennia after the fall, the lament of the psalmist is heard in a different language. Poetic expression has given way to controlled trials and metanalyses, yet they describe the same loss. The fracture now undulates with seismic force—within individual lives, in broken relationships, and across entire systems. Nowhere is this more evident than in modern medicine, where disintegration has taken painfully tangible shape: the human person—and even illness itself—fragmented into parts, managed by teams of specialists, coded diagnoses, and algorithmic care pathways. Even our most basic medical rituals reflect this divide. The patient history routinely parses spiritual, mental, and physical health into separate inquiries, as if they exist in isolation from one another. What was once nephesh—an integrated soul—is now divided among cardiologists, pulmonologists, psychiatrists, and chaplains.

This is not a concern to be relegated to theologians and philosophers

---

1   Blaise Pascal, *Blaise Pascal's Pensées* (Penguin Books, 1966), 75. *Pensées* was originally published by a team of French scholars in 1670.

alone. The consequences of fragmentation are well documented in clinical literature and carry measurable implications for patient care. A 2007 study found that the average Medicare patient sees two primary care providers and five specialists over a two-year span.[2] For these medically complex individuals with multiple chronic conditions, this kind of fractured care contributes to diminished quality, inefficiency, and even harm—particularly through the overutilization of emergency departments and diagnostic testing.[3] Medication errors, preventable hospitalizations, and departures from best medical practices all become more frequent when a whole person is divided by systems of care.[4] Tangible, systemic echoes of the fall, some reinforcing the schism within, often causing physical harm. Missed medication reconciliations lead to dangerous interactions. Duplicated testing exposes patients to unnecessary radiation, risk, or cost. Fragmented follow up leads to avoidable hospital readmissions.

But just as described in Genesis, this disintegration is not merely systemic: East of Eden, it exists within us. Modern trauma literature echoes this with the same painful clarity found in the story of leaving the garden. Unprocessed pain does not simply disappear—it embeds itself somatically, relationally, spiritually.

The body carrying trauma as chronic pain, digestive disorders, or autoimmune flares.

Isolation from those who long to help because trust seems impossible.

An inability to pray, as silence feels unsafe.

---

2   Hoangmai H. Pham, Deborah Schrag, et al., "Care Patterns in Medicare and Their Implications for Pay for Performance," *New England Journal of Medicine* 356, no. 11 (2007): 1130–39.

3   Jee Young Joo, "Fragmented Care and Chronic Illness Patient Outcomes: A Systematic Review," *Nursing Open* 10, no. 6 (2023): 3460–73, https://doi.org/10.1002/nop2.1607.

4   Edward Chang, Sanjay Basu, et al, "Care Fragmentation, Quality, and Costs Among Chronically Ill Patients," *American Journal of Managed Care*, May 2023, https://www.ajmc.com/view/care-fragmentation-quality-costs-among-chronically-ill-patients.

Trauma, as noted by Bessel van der Kolk in his book *The Body Keeps the Score*, is not simply remembered as a story—it is relived as a reaction.[5] It leaves no tidy trail. Instead, it splinters time, confuses memory, and disrupts the body's natural rhythm. The traumatized self struggles to feel safe in its own skin—cut off from sensation, from trust, from rest. In a fractured nephesh, the body no longer testifies to God's peace but instead reacts to fear. Even as the soul clings to truths it believes, the body flinches, dissociates, tightens its grip on its share of the self. What was once fluid and whole becomes like a shattered mirror—each shard reflecting some part of the image but none revealing the fullness. What God designed to be unified now scrambles to survive moment by moment.

Trauma bears witness to the disruption of the nephesh: woundedness permeating every facet of what God designed to be integrated, complementary, whole. Even fresh pain reverberates with echoes of something more ancient. Awaiting biopsy results stings with more than mere prognostic uncertainty; it reawakens the fear of mortality that has haunted humanity since the fall. The body crippled by arthritis, still burdened by vocation, longs for the joyful labor once given in Eden. In the silence of an empty house, the fresh grief of widowhood awakens a deeper longing—the intimacy of the Triune love in which we were first made. These manifestations testify not only to the depth of our fracture but to the profound sanctity of the preserved living soul—the nephesh—which God still intends to restore.

Today, humanity is not without awareness of this pain. Movements within—and especially alongside—modern medicine themselves bear witness to a longing for restoration, for return within us. The surge of interest in biohacking, integrative care, mindfulness, trauma-informed

---

5   Bessel van der Kolk, *The Body Keeps the Score: Brain, Mind, and Body in the Healing of Trauma* (Viking, 2014), 17.

therapy, and functional medicine points to this deeper yearning.[6] We long for a model that honors the unity of the human person.

We are searching for Eden without always knowing it. In every algorithm, supplement, self-tracking app, and guided meditation, there is an ache for wholeness—a distant echo of nephesh, still calling us home.

The fracture is real. It is spiritual, relational, and embodied. Our profound yearning for wholeness testifies to its reach. Its echoes permeate every fiber of our being—the pain of the fall weaving through DNA, organs, minds, relationships, even the very systems meant to heal. It plays out in the dissonance of our habits, the strain of our relationships, the fragmentation of how we care for the hurt. What was once whole has been scattered. The nephesh—body and breath, form and meaning—buckles under the weight of disintegration.

And yet God has not withdrawn from what is broken. Even now, beyond the garden, the Breath-Giver draws near. He walks among the rubble. He still asks, *Where are you?*—not out of unknowing but because He *longs* for us to see where we've hidden, where we've hurt, where we've split. His presence is not reserved for the integrated; it permeates the broken. He draws nearer still to those who are fractured (Psalm 34:18).

This is not the end of our story.

But to begin the work of restoration, we must ask: How did we arrive here? How have we numbed or distracted ourselves from the pain of the fracture? What lenses have shaped how we see ourselves? What cultural, clinical, philosophical, and spiritual frameworks have defined our understanding of health, healing—even the soul?

Before we can invite the Creator to mend what is broken, we must first unmask the false frameworks that have made fragmentation feel normal.

---

6   Biohacking refers to do-it-yourself approaches to health that combine technology, biology, and personal experimentation. Mindfulness is the practice of paying attention, without judgment, to the present moment. Trauma-informed therapy emphasizes safety and trust in the healing process. Functional medicine seeks to address root causes of illness rather than symptoms.

NEPHESH LIVING

Pause here.

Take a slow breath in: *You are near to the broken.*

And out: *Here I am, Lord.*

You are not hidden from the Breath-Giver.

He walks among the broken.

He asks, still: *Where are you?*

REFLECTION: FEELING THE FRACTURE

- Where do you feel the echoes of the fracture in your own life?

- Where do you sense disintegration—between what you believe and how you live, between what your body needs and what your habits allow, between your longing for connection and your daily experience?

- Notice the places where your nephesh feels divided. Not with shame. With honesty. With kindness.

- Can you name the adaptations that have helped you survive—but kept you living in pieces?

- Can you trace the frameworks—spoken or unspoken—that have taught you healing means performance, that soul care is secondary, that being whole is someone else's talent or calling?

MAY THE RECOGNITION OF YOUR FRACTURES AWAKEN HOPE–

THE DEEP YEARNING FOR A LIFE MADE WHOLE.

3

THE FALSE FRAMEWORK

The eye is the lamp of the body. So, if your eye is healthy, your whole body will be full of light; but if your eye is bad, your whole body will be full of darkness.

MATTHEW 6:22-23 ESV

A CIVIL ENGINEER, presenting for routine follow-up. The binder he typically brought with pride was there, as always—meticulously organized with blood pressure logs, daily blood sugars, and recorded weights. He was articulate, well read, and sincerely committed to his health. But today his usual confidence was absent.

Visibly frustrated, he shared his discouragement. "I've done everything right. Everything." A flush crept into his cheeks. "I've taken my supplements, meditated, tracked macros, tithed, exercised daily. My labs are the best they've ever been. But I don't feel better. I feel like I keep coming up short of how I know I should feel."

His effort wasn't the problem. His disorientation came from faithfully living out a model that didn't heal. The systems he trusted delivered data but not healing. The framework he followed sold the illusion of change, yet nothing truly moved. And the ache beneath it all whispered what he hadn't yet dared to name: Maybe the framework itself was false.

He isn't alone.

Anchored in the truth of Scripture, it isn't difficult to recognize that we are fractured. But the question begs to be asked: Why do we live this way? Who told us this was normal? Why have we settled for less?

Whether or not we're aware of it, we all operate within assumed frameworks. These are inherited and absorbed—often silently, without notice. Many are cultural: performance, independence, the curated self. Some are clinical: the body as a machine to be optimized, pain as a number to be managed, healing as compliance. Others are theological: a gospel with little regard for the body, over-spiritualized.

Each of these becomes a lens that distorts our worldview and sense of self. But they are not mere abstractions or passing philosophies. They are a trellis—subtle but sturdy—upon which our identity and our understanding of wholeness are trained to grow. Our instincts are recalibrated: what to notice, what to ignore; what to value, what to dismiss; what to nurture, what to override. They foster striving and normalize compartmentalization. And over time they convince us that living scattered is the price of being good or strong or faithful.

The false framework does not arrive with a black-box warning. It is learned by repetition, absorbed through expectation, lived as though it were truth.

These frameworks do not simply reflect the fracture.

They *reinforce it.*

But these frameworks are not new.

Long before the rise of the self-help book or the disintegration of modern health systems, they were planted in the fragile soil of our collective imagination by a different story, a different understanding. One in which the soul and the body were not united in wholeness but cast as rivals. In conflict.

In Scripture, the nephesh—made in God's image, echoing His triune wholeness, called "good" by God Himself—stood as His ultimate creation. Dust and breath, woven together in sacred rhythm. In the garden there was no hierarchy of parts, no suspicion of the physical body. All moved as one: the spirit elevating and offering the body before God; the body moving in step with the spirit and the pulse of the Breath-Giver. There was no conflict within. No impulse to transcend the physical in order to access the spiritual.

There was only integration. Belonging—in one's own flesh, in relationship, and in the presence of God.

But as the ripples of the fall pressed us further and further east of Eden, a new narrative emerged. As in the garden, the voice of deception was subtle but alluring. This time it didn't just cast doubt on God's goodness but on the goodness of the body itself. A vision that framed the physical as flawed, disposable, inferior, while the soul was elevated as pure, eternal, and divine.

Plato gave voice to this vision. In his framework, the soul was the true self: eternal, transcendent, untouchable. The body, by contrast, was a prison—earthly, unclean, and fleeting. The goal of life, he taught, was to escape it, to ascend out of the realm of flesh and into a world of perfect, abstract forms. In Plato's imagination, the spiritual was not just different from the physical. It was separate. It was superior.[1]

These ideas, though philosophical, soon found theological expression. In the first centuries of the church, a heretical movement known as Gnosticism taught that the material world had been created by a lesser, corrupted god—and that salvation came through secret spiritual knowledge, enabling the soul to escape the body. The early church rightly condemned this vision. But its residue lingered. The body became suspect. The soul became supreme. And disintegration seeped

---

1   Plato, *Phaedo*, 81b–84b, trans. R. S. Bluck, in *Plato's Phaedo: A Translation of Plato's Phaedo with Introduction, Notes and Appendices* (Routledge, 2000), 80–84.

deeper into the church's spiritual imagination.[2]

Some early Christian thinkers, like Origen and Augustine, were faithful in their devotion to Christ and explicit in their rejection of Gnostic teaching.[3] Yet even they were shaped by the philosophical categories of their age—especially those drawn from Plato. The soul became the seat of salvation; the body the source of sin—not in the biblical sense of "the flesh," but in the Greek philosophical sense that the material realm itself was morally suspect. The sacred was exalted. The material regarded with distrust.

This wasn't always explicit, but it reshaped the church's spiritual imagination for generations. The Word became flesh—but Christian practice often lived as though He hadn't. We spoke of bodily resurrection yet lived as though salvation meant escape. We pursued sanctification as though only the soul mattered, while viewing the body as disposable — something to be shed at death rather than a temple destined for glory. In doing so, we neglected the stewardship of our physical lives, forgetting that these very bodies will one day be raised, redeemed, and glorified.

The tide slowly eroded the wholeness once found in Eden. We forgot God's design for fully integrated nephesh living. We preached resurrection but lived as disembodied souls. We entrusted our spirits to Jesus but struggled to inhabit the bodies His Father called good. We lamented the weakness of the flesh while quietly abandoning its sacredness.

Plato's framework dissected the soul from the body, but it was René Descartes who took the next decisive step—dividing the mind from everything else. Writing much later, in the seventeenth century, he sought certainty in an increasingly uncertain world. Perhaps most

---

2   Lars P. Qualben, *A History of the Christian Church* (Wipf and Stock, 2008), 78.

3   Jason BeDuhn, *Augustine's Manichaean Dilemma, Volume 2: Making a "Catholic," Self, 388–401 C.E.* (University of Pennsylvania Press, 2013), 196.

concretely, he declared the foundation of his vision *Cogito, ergo sum*. I think, therefore I am.[4]

In this framework, the thinking mind became the seat of identity. The body was no longer integral to personhood but incidental to it—a tool, a vessel, a machine. Descartes didn't just separate spirit from flesh—he severed reason from sensation, the measurable from the meaningful. And though he contributed greatly to the development of rigorous Christian thought, his vision deepened the fracture within God's original design for the integrated, living soul.

The effects were profound.

Within Christianity the sacred grew increasingly disconnected from the material. But this legacy of disintegration didn't remain in the musings of philosophers and theologians—it shaped entire systems. In medicine, Descartes's vision laid the groundwork for the body to be treated as an object—something to be examined, diagnosed, and fixed. It formed the very system in which I practice. The physician became marked by what Michel Foucault would later call "the clinical gaze": trained not to see personhood but pathology.[5]

Like Descartes's own philosophy, this lens was not malicious. It was efficient, well intentioned, designed to keep pace with our growing knowledge of disease. It made patient care precise. Predictable. But it came at a cost. That which could not be measured—grief, hope, meaning, the matters of the living soul—was often overlooked or unexamined. Presence was replaced by protocol. Wholeness gave way to parts.

When Mr. Jones—husband, grandfather, retired airline pilot, backyard barbecue master—becomes "68-year-old African American male with a history of type 2 diabetes, hypertension, and coronary artery

---

4   René Descartes, *Meditations on First Philosophy*, trans. John Cottingham (Cambridge University Press, 1996), 17.

5   Michel Foucault, *The Birth of the Clinic: An Archaeology of Medical Perception*, trans. A. M. Sheridan (New York: Vintage Books, 1994), 107–8.

disease," the beholding of a nephesh, the sacred unity beneath the symptoms, is lost.

When we diagnose a patient with cancer but do not witness their suffering ...

When we consider review of systems but not spiritual distress ...

When we recall a chart but forget a life ...

We are living out the inheritance of the clinical gaze.

In daily life, Decartes's framework reinforced the belief that wellness meant mastery over the body through intellect—that we must rise above feeling and prioritize performance over presence.

We see this today in our homes, our watches, our mirrors. We measure and track sleep scores, glucose trends, heart rate zones, macros—all in the name of optimization. Not to become whole but to become better. Sharper. Leaner. More in control. We treat our bodies not as living souls but as machines to be tuned.

Even within the church we adopt spiritual language to describe the same syndrome: discipline, excellence, stewardship. But too often we slip into the same old framework—the body as obstacle to the spirit, hunger as distraction, emotion as threat. Weakness is not to be healed but rebuked.

Like dust divorced from breath, we become divided against ourselves—praying our way through anxiety while scrolling and caffeinating through exhaustion. Longing for God's peace while punishing our bodies into submission. Trying to be whole while still living in parts.

This is not new. It is the inherited ache of a long, slow unraveling—one that began with the severing of soul from body, mind from matter, person from self. The rift, once imagined in philosophy, became lived reality. And in many ways, that fracture still shapes us today.

But inheritance is not destiny.

We are not bound to repeat what we've received.

Scripture names this act of refusal and return as *repentance*—not a word of shame but of courage. A holy turning—from the lies that dismember the body, not from the body itself. Not from our humanity but from the frameworks that hollow it out. To repent is to say, "I will no longer live divided. I will no longer mistake management for healing. I will come back."

And in that return, the Breath-Giver meets us. Not with rebuke but restoration.

Not with reprimand but with a robe. A ring. A feast.

The fracture is not final.

The story that began in dust and breath does not end in separation. The Breath-Giver has not abandoned His most cherished creation. Jesus shows us the fullness of God *and* the fullness of what it means to be human. He did not come to rescue us from embodiment but to redeem it.

His gaze was different—searching far beyond physical symptoms. He recognized that the lame first needed forgiveness of sin; the outcast tax collector, relational restoration; the bleeding woman, dignity and belonging.

He healed lepers. He wept at tombs. He broke bread with the weary and washed the feet of the worn. In Him body and spirit moved in harmony once more.

The way of Jesus is incarnation, not escape.

Embodied love, not disembodied striving.

And through Him the invitation still stands: to be made whole again.[6]

---

6   For readers who want to explore how this fracture took root in the very words used to translate Scripture—how *nephesh* became "psyche" and "soma," and why that matters—see appendix E: "Why Words Matter." It offers a brief but important reflection on how our language has shaped the Christian imagination, often in ways that reinforce the very fragmentation Christ came to heal.

Pause here.

Take note of any aches, tensions, uncomfortable questions.

Ask God to search your heart. Allow yourself to be honest.

Take a slow breath in: *You knit me together.*

And breathe out: *Restore me to wholeness.*

Jesus did not call disembodied souls.

He called fishermen, tax collectors, women, children—the weary and broken.

He still calls you.

Not to strive harder but to come home.

REFLECTION: UNMASKING THE FRAMEWORK

- How do you define wholeness? Where have you inherited assumptions about what it means to be whole?

- What unspoken beliefs shape how you measure health, faithfulness, or worth?

- Can you identify frameworks in your own life—clinical, cultural, theological—that have taught you to separate soul from body, intellect from emotion?

- In what parts of your life have you settled for management instead of healing?

- Where have you substituted optimization for wholeness?

MAY YOU LAY ASIDE WHAT FRACTURES AND DISTORTS,

AND MAY YOUR SOUL FIND REST AGAIN IN THE WHOLENESS

OF GOD'S DESIGN.

4

A RETURN TO EDEN

Come to me, all you who are weary and burdened, and I will give you rest ...
For my yoke is easy and my burden is light.

MATTHEW 11:28-30

HE FILLED THE DOORFRAME—broad shouldered, long bearded, draped in tattoos—as my nurse led him into the exam room for his first visit with me. After she completed her intake, she gave me a familiar "good luck" glance on her way out, and I stepped in behind her.

His presence was striking. Even his fingers bore ink—bony phalanx tattoos traced over each one, like a skeleton reaching outward. Everything about him projected toughness. Trauma. Violence.

But when he sat down, his voice was soft. "Just got out." He rested his hands heavily on his knees. "Ten years."

At first he didn't say much else, as if he had to consciously set aside the identity he'd worn as a federal inmate. Eventually he told me he'd been part of a drug-running operation connected to the Hell's Angels. The story was long, marked by choices he didn't excuse but no longer clung to.

"I found Jesus in there." He tapped his chest with a thick finger. "Changed everything."

He said it plainly—without polish or performance. Though he'd clearly told this story before, it hadn't grown rehearsed. He spoke with the weight of someone who at his lowest point had met God—and believed Him.

He got clean. Lost weight. Led Bible studies behind bars. Started a ministry for other inmates still serving time. But what mattered most— what brought a smile across his tattooed, scarred, sun-worn face—was his daughter.

"She answers my calls now." His voice caught. "She even came to see me."

For all his size and his story, what lingered most after he'd left wasn't his past or appearance. It was his softness. His healed presence.

What the world had once dismissed as dangerous, Jesus had called beloved.

What was shattered had begun to mend.

"He breathed on them and said, 'Receive the Holy Spirit.'"

JOHN 20:22

This was not the first time God had breathed life into dust. The first breath had made humanity. This one would remake them.

The Greek word used here—*enephysēsen* (ἐνεφύσησεν)—is "striking." It appears only once in the New Testament, here in John 20:22. And its only other occurrence in all of Scripture is in the Greek translation of Genesis 2:7, when God breathes life into Adam.

This was not coincidence. It was re-creation. The same breath that animated the dust of Eden was now exhaled again—through the resurrected Christ, into His disciples—not just forming life but restoring it.

In the garden God's breath had animated dust into nephesh—whole, living souls. But here, in the quiet after resurrection, Jesus stood before His disciples—bearing the memory of wounds, yet risen—and *breathed*. It wasn't symbolic. It was renewal. The Breath-Giver exhaled once more. The divine rhythm resumed. The Spirit was being poured not just *on* them but *into* them.

It was the beginning of wholeness—again.

This moment, often overlooked for its brevity, is the hinge upon which the entire story turns—not just the story of Scripture but our story. Yours. Mine. Every fractured soul longing to become whole again. The life Jesus offers isn't a distant hope reserved for the end of days. It is here. It is now. It is breathed.

Wholeness returns not in thunder or spectacle but in breath. In presence. In wounds not erased but redeemed. In the quiet giving of the same Spirit who once hovered over creation—and now dwells within.

This is the way of Jesus.

THE WHOLENESS OF SALVATION

This way of wholeness—the invitation not just to forgiveness but to life restored—echoes deeply in the ancient language of faith.

In Greek the word we translate as "salvation" is *sōtēria* (σωτηρία). It means more than rescue or a promise of heaven. It carries the weight of being made whole—of healing, preservation, and renewal. Derived from *sōzō* (σῴζω), it speaks of saving *and* restoring. It's the same word used in the Gospels when Jesus heals the woman who touched His cloak: "Your faith has made you well" (Luke 8:48 ESV). In Greek it reads, "Your faith has saved you." *Sōzō*.

Salvation, then, is not a disembodied transaction. It is the healing of nephesh—the reintegration of the whole person, breath and body, spirit and flesh.

The story of Jesus's breath in John 20:22 was more than a symbolic act—it was re-creation. In breathing the Spirit upon His disciples, He was not simply granting them access to heaven; He was renewing the life they were made for. To receive *sōtēria* is to return to the wholeness of our original design.

In this new life, we no longer live as fractured souls waiting for escape but as restored beings drawn into God's own life—breathing His breath, embodying His love, participating in His fullness. Salvation is both future hope and present reality—a wholeness that touches the body, heals the mind, and reconciles the heart.

This is not a new teaching. It's as ancient as God's breath over dust in the garden.

As enduring as His covenant faithfulness.

As intimate as His touch on leprous skin.

Sōtēria is wholeness given and received, not earned or achieved.

And it is still being offered.

BREATHING AS RESTORATION

This way of salvation—*sōtēria*—restores us not only to wholeness in the abstract but to the integrated, sacred rhythm of life itself. It calls us back to our breath.

Mindfulness teachers and health experts extol the benefits of slow, deliberate breathing. Techniques like box breathing and diaphragmatic breathing have been shown to reduce anxiety, help lower blood pressure, and improve focus.[1] But these are not new. They are echoes.

The first breath was God's. Genesis tells us that He breathed into dust, animating it into a living nephesh—a whole, living soul. Every breath we take is a continuation of that moment, a rhythmic reminder of our origin and our dependence on the Breath-Giver.

When Jesus breathed on His disciples in John 20:22, He was not performing a spiritual ritual detached from reality. He was restoring the

---

1   Balban, Muhammed Y., et al. "Brief Structured Respiration Practices Enhance Mood and Reduce Physiological Arousal." *Cell Reports Medicine* 4, no. 2 (February 21, 2023): 100936. https://doi.org/10.1016/j.xcrm.2023.100936

breath of creation itself. His exhalation was both a symbol and a reality: the Spirit filling not just their lungs but their whole selves, reanimating their nephesh with divine presence.

In a world filled with shallow, hurried breaths—racing from task to task, suppressing stress, numbing our senses—the invitation of *sōtēria* is to pause. To breathe deeply. To remember.

Modern breathing practices may regulate our nervous systems, but they also have the potential to sync us with the deeper truth: that we are created beings, drawing life from God with every inhale and exhaling praise with every breath out. In Acts 17:25 Paul proclaims that "He Himself gives everyone life and breath and everything else." And Psalm 150:6 calls out this: "Let everything that has breath praise the LORD."

Our breathing is more than physiological regulation—it is worship. Surrender. A daily reminder, carried in our very breath and bodies, that we were made for wholeness and that wholeness begins with remembering whose breath fills us.

THE HEALING GAZE

With Jesus came something new: a different kind of gaze.

The woman at the well did not leave changed because He explained her sin. She left changed because He *saw* her.

The bleeding woman did not press through the crowd for theological exposition, to grow in knowledge. She came because she believed—even if only in desperation—that if she could just touch Him, healing would happen. And when He turned to face her, His eyes didn't flash with indignation or scrutiny.

He called her "daughter."

Time and again,

the gaze of Jesus offers what no diagnosis, no algorithm, no framework ever could: restoration through recognition. Where the clinical gaze fragments, the eyes of Jesus make whole. He sees the person, not the parts. The story, not just the symptoms.

Jesus did not come to offer a theory or method of wholeness. He came to offer it through redemption.

In Him there was no fracture. No dissonance between word and action, soul and flesh, presence and power. His body bore the fullness of divinity, not symbolically but fully, truly (Colossians 2:9). And through that body, he dwelled among us. He broke bread with us. He drew near to the leper whom no one else would. He received oil on His feet and tears on His skin. He healed through proximity. With breath. With touch.

And in doing so, He gave the world a Savior but also a vision—a lens through which to reinterpret our fractured framework. He became the living example—the wholeness we were made for and the wholeness we are invited to live once more.

In Jesus, wholeness was never the reward of achievement or perfection, something to be earned. It was the fruit of love.

HEALING AS INTEGRATION

But what exactly does it look like to be healed? To be whole?

In medicine healing is too often reduced to resolution—of disease, of pain, of disability. But the way of Jesus resists this reductionist view. In John 9 Jesus's disciples ask, upon seeing a man blind from birth, "Who sinned, this man or his parents?" (v. 2). They were drawing from the ancient—and still common—assumption that suffering is always the consequence of wrongdoing and that healing means its reversal.

Jesus's answer is clear, piercing, and filled with grace: "Neither this man nor his parents sinned ... but this happened so that the works of God might be displayed in Him" (v. 3). His words decouple illness from blame and healing from simple restoration back to a previous or idealized state.

The man's blindness was not punishment. His healing was not merit. The purpose of both was glory. His story was not a tragedy to erase but a testimony through which God would be revealed.

This reorients us entirely. In Jesus's framework, healing does not always mean the elimination of symptoms. It is the unveiling of presence—God's presence within the body, even (and perhaps demonstrably through) its limitations. Wholeness is found in proximity to the Breath-Giver, not perfection. Healing is not always synonymous with cure. For the living soul, healing may look like forgiveness. Like dignity. Like connection.

Modern clinical literature echoes this truth. Studies consistently show that the quality of the patient-provider relationship—especially when marked by empathy and presence—can measurably improve health outcomes, sometimes rivaling or surpassing traditional interventions.[2]

And the same principle holds beyond the exam room. Participation in spiritual community—especially through regular worship—has been associated with lower mortality rates, reduced depression, and greater life satisfaction, even after accounting for lifestyle and demographic differences.[3]

These findings may be voiced through modern language, but they are not new. The evidence affirms what Jesus revealed from the very beginning: Healing is found in presence, not detachment. Among Jesus, among others. Flourishing is produced through meaning, not by metrics. From the woman at the well to the leper on the roadside, Jesus healed through power and through proximity.

Dignity restored, community reintegrated, people called by name.

---

2 John M. Kelley, Gordon Kraft-Todd G, et al., "The Influence of the Patient-Clinician Relationship on Healthcare Outcomes: A Systematic Review and Meta-Analysis of Randomized Controlled Trials," PLOS One 9, no. 6, (2014): e1101191, https://doi.org/10.1371/journal.pone.0094207. Also, D. P. Rakel DP, T. J. Hoeft, et al., "Physician Empathy and Chronic Pain Outcomes," JAMA Network Open 6, no. 3 (2023): e235980, https://jamanetworkopen/fullarticle/2817441.

3 S. Li, M. J. Stampfer, et al., "Association of Religious Service Attendance with Mortality Among Women," JAMA Internal Medicine, no 6., vol. 176 (2016): 777–85, https://doi.org/10.1001/jamainternmed.2016.1615.

The data reveal to us what the Gospels have already shown: People are changed when they are seen, known, and loved. Wholeness unfolds in communion. It is discovered in abiding, not in striving. The path to restoration often begins with presence, not with a prescription.

But presence is only the beginning.

The way of Jesus shows us that healing also looks like renewed integration. If the fracture scattered the spheres of our being—spiritual, physical, relational—so they ran in parallel but never intersected, then wholeness in Jesus is their restoration: the reweaving of what was torn. The same breath that filled the disciples with the Spirit—the very breath that raised Jesus from the dead (Romans 8:11)—now lives within us.

When that truth becomes our north star, everything changes.

Work becomes worship.

Nutrition becomes an offering at the temple of our body.

Exercise becomes Edenic—fulfilling, not depleting.

Relationship becomes reflection of the Trinity.

And our days become nephesh: joyful submission lived in the body at the altar of His feet.

This kind of wholeness isn't theoretical—it's transformational. It recalibrates how we live: not hustling to become something else but resting in who we were always meant to be. Integration restores our inner belonging. We no longer live in conflict with ourselves. Instead, we are aligned—body, mind, and spirit—in the quiet strength of being fully known and fully loved.

This is an invitation to unity, not hyper-discipline or spiritualized optimization. A life no longer pulled in competing directions. One lived as a whole soul—restored, reconnected, reanimated.

This is the way of Jesus: near, personal, integrated. The Breath-Giver draws close to our fractured selves, not with a diagnosis but with wholeness. When we put aside our striving—set down the false frameworks we've carried—and take Jesus at His word, a new invitation unfolds.

He does not merely ask us to believe. He asks us to come. To receive healing. To receive rest. And as we come, we begin to see that the heaviness we carry is layered—pressed upon us from the world and borne also from the fractures within.

We were not made to live in pieces. We were made to live as living souls—fully human, fully known, fully whole.

In Him the weight becomes light. The yoke easy. The burden no longer ours to bear alone.

This is the invitation of Jesus:

to cease striving,

to live fuller,

to be made whole again.

Receive it now.

Pause here.

Breathe in: *The Breath-Giver is near.*

Breathe out: *And He makes all things whole.*

Wholeness does not begin with striving.

It begins with coming.

With being seen.

With being loved.

Let your soul rest there.

REFLECTION: WHOLENESS RESTORED

- Where have you experienced the gaze of Jesus—not as scrutiny but as love? In what parts of your life do you resist this?

- Where have you mistaken disconnection for discipline? Performance for faithfulness?

- Are there places in your life where you have treated your body as something to conquer or silence rather than a temple to honor?

- What spheres of your life—physical, emotional, relational, spiritual—have been running in parallel but not in harmony?

MAY THE BREATH OF CHRIST, ECHOING THE FIRST BREATH IN EDEN, RENEW YOU AND RESTORE YOU TO THE WHOLENESS OF LIVING NEPHESH.

PART II

THE FORMATION: LEARNING TO LIVE WHOLE AGAIN

5

WHAT IS LIVING NEPHESH?

He restores my soul. He leads me in paths of righteousness for his name's sake.
PSALM 23:3 ESV

SHE SAID IT WITHOUT FANFARE. No histrionics. No hint of needing affirmation. Just a quiet statement of fact as she sat on the edge of the exam table, a chipped pink fingernail tapping the medication list she'd finally kept consistent for months.

"I'm better now," she repeated. "Messy still, but better."

And she was. Not perfect—not even close. But more whole.

The first time she came into my clinic, it was chaos: weeping, manic, slurred speech from the night before. Eight children. Half a dozen fathers. A string of one-night stands tied to the swinging arc of bipolar disorder and substance use. She never stayed long at any job. Never came back for follow-up. Never remembered which pharmacy she used

And yet ...

One visit, she was different. Calmer. Slower.

She shared that she had found a church that made her feel seen. She had been sober for two months. She had started reading Proverbs, just one line a day. Said her son prayed over dinner now.

It wasn't instant, and it wasn't easy. She still forgot appointments. Still missed doses. Still had to fight off the pull of old patterns and old companions.

But over time—months, not days—she steadied.

She kept the same job. Kept her follow-ups. Smiled without the jagged edge of fear behind it.

She asked questions about her care. Advocated for her own mental health. Learned to say no. Learned to stay. Learned to be a mother who was present, not just surviving.

She was still tired. Still single. Still had kids who tested her patience. Still had cravings for drugs and alcohol. But she was there. Alive. Healing. Living.

Not perfect. But better.

"I'm better now. Messy still, but better."

Her words weren't a declaration of victory but a quiet testimony of becoming. Of movement. Of healing that didn't arrive all at once but slowly took shape—over months, over prayers, over pills faithfully taken and bottles finally left unopened.

What unfolded in her life was more than sobriety or symptom control. It was integration. Her story reminds us that wholeness is more than survival or management—it's the slow knitting back together of what once came undone. The rediscovery of what it means to live as a *living soul*—loving God with all her heart, her soul, her strength.

Scripture doesn't invite compartmentalized devotion or isolated disciplines but a life lived whole before God. In the *Shema*—the ancient prayer still recited daily by millions—God calls His people to love Him with every fiber of who they are. Not one part held back. Not one part cast off.

What does that look like today? And how do we begin to live that way—on our best days as well as in the chaos of the ordinary? This chapter is about defining what it means to be a living nephesh—and learning to walk in that identity—one integrated, grace-filled step at a time.

SHEMA: THE FRAMEWORK FOR WHOLENESS

"Hear, O Israel: The LORD our God, the LORD is one" (Deuteronomy 6:4–5). So begins the Shema—Israel's central declaration of faith and its call to love the Lord with all one's heart, soul (nephesh), and strength. These words were, and still are, foundational for the Hebrew people. Chief among the verses committed to memory by Jewish children, they formed the bedrock of identity and devotion.

Jesus Himself, when asked to name the greatest commandment, turned to this very passage. In Mark He echoed it—adding a call to love one's neighbor—and declared it the most essential of all commandments (Mark 12:29–31). His emphasis invites our careful attention.

In Hebrew understanding, the Shema's three words encompass the fullness of human life. *Lebab* (heart) refers to emotion but also implies the will, intention, and the inner person. *Nephesh* (soul) means life itself—an embodied, breathing self. *Me'od* (commonly translated "strength") conveys the idea of "muchness"—one's energy, wealth, resources, and capacities.[1] To love God with all our heart, soul, and strength is to love Him with everything. Every thought, word, gesture, and act becomes worship.

This is the framework of living nephesh: fully integrated devotion. Not a fragmented spiritual practice but whole-person love. Not compartmentalized duty but worship made visible in every sphere of life.

---

1   Tim Mackie, "What's the Meaning of the Jewish Shema Prayer in the Bible?," BibleProject, February 18, 2017, https://bibleproject.com/articles/what-is-the-shema/.

A LIVING SOUL REVISITED

In Genesis 2, the first nephesh was brought to life as God breathed into dust (Genesis 2:7). That same word—*nephesh*—is what the Shema now invites us to love God with: not just a spirit but a whole person—undivided, fully alive.

In Hebrew thought there was no divide between body and spirit, no artificial separation of spiritual life from daily life. *Nephesh* meant the entire person—breathing, hungering, laboring, worshiping. Here in Deuteronomy's most foundational command, the vision of whole-person living comes full circle: The one who was formed by God's breath is now called to love God with all they are.

This is what it means to live as a living nephesh.

NEPHESH: MORE THAN A SOUL

Best understood as "life" or a "whole person," the Hebrew word *nephesh* does not suggest an immortal, ghostlike essence floating free from the body. Instead, as one theologian notes, its Old Testament meaning is "simply organic life"—a fully lived existence.[2] In Genesis 2:7 God breathes into the dust, and the human becomes a living nephesh—not a soul trapped in a body, but a unified, breathing being.

This is the foundational vision of humanity in Scripture: body and spirit in communion, not competition. Wholeness by design. Integration from the start.

Paul echoes this vision in 1 Thessalonians 5:23, where he prays that

---

2   J. Richard Middleton, "Paul on the 'Soul'—Not What You Might Think," *Creation to Eschaton*, October 23, 2014, https://jrichardmiddleton.com/2014/10/23/paul-on-the-soul-not-what-you-might-think/.

the spirit, soul, and body be kept blameless and whole. His words carry theological weight, but they also offer a practical invitation—to view our entire selves as sacred, each part belonging to God.

Living nephesh, then, is not an abstract idea. It means honoring our emotions, our choices, our physicality, our presence in the world—as one seamless expression of devotion.

This stands in sharp contrast to the later dualism of Greek thought, which separated soul from body and spiritual from physical. But the Genesis story paints no such divide. God calls the embodied life "very good." In the psalms, bones rejoice and hearts reason. In this tradition worship belongs to the whole person, not intellect alone—breath, body, longing, and song.

To be a nephesh is to be alive to God—in every part of who we are.

It is the life that Jesus invites us into—in eternity, but also here and now: "I have come that they may have life, and have it to the full" (John 10:10).

This is not merely a call to survive or even to integrate, but to participate. The ancient church called this *theosis*—a word that means becoming one with God's life. Peter writes "that through [these promises] you may become partakers of the divine nature" (2 Peter 1:4 ESV). Living nephesh, at its heart, is about more than healing what is broken.

It is about being drawn into the divine life of God Himself. It is a restoration of the life we were created for, in communion with the Breath-Giver.

RECOGNIZING THE FRACTURE

Given that this was God's intended design for us, we all live with a deeply embedded calling back to wholeness—however repressed or diluted it may be. Our nephesh can be fractured by sin, trauma, illness, or all of those. And because God created us with the capacity to adapt, the signs of a shattered soul are often dangerously subtle: disjointed desires, constant inner conflict, emotional numbness. Like Adam and Eve in the garden, we instinctively hide. Our conscience buries these warning signs in shame or self-protection.

But the path toward restoration depends not on our own self-discovery—it is a Spirit-led unveiling. Purposeful, prayerful leaning into God is essential for illuminating these hidden fractures.

A fractured soul may ignore God's voice, misuse one's strength, or live out of sync: patterns of bingeing, isolation, self-harm, or overdependence on work, substances, or relationships for identity and worth. This way of living is the opposite of Shema life—where love for God flows from all of who we are.

By contrast, God invites us into something far richer. **The integrated soul is living nephesh: a person whose heart, mind, and body work together under the reign of God's love.** From the Shema onward, Scripture calls us to a devotion that includes every faculty—nothing withheld or compartmentalized.

The healed heart is honest and whole. The mind is attuned to God's wisdom. Strength is managed with responsibility and integrity. These are not independent virtues but interwoven graces. Like the triune nature of the God who made us, the components of our being are meant to function in communion—with one another and with Him.

As the psalmist prays in Psalm 51, the result is a clean heart and a right spirit. In the integrated nephesh, thoughts, emotions, and actions flow from one stream of grace—restored, aligned, and alive.

LIVING NEPHESH IN PRACTICE

While healing and wholeness—the restoration of the living soul—are ultimately gifts from God, unearned yet inherited, Scripture also implies a human response. As Paul writes, we are to "work out [our] own salvation with fear and trembling, for it is God who works in [us] to will and to act in order to fulfill his good purpose" (Philippians 2:12–13). We are invited to move toward what we've been given. To receive wholeness, we must participate in it.

That movement begins with discernment. First, living as a whole soul requires self-awareness and Spirit-led perception. Discernment helps us recognize when something is misaligned—when our hearts stray from peace or our bodies bear the signs of burden. It allows us to distinguish the stirrings of God from the pull of ego. It reveals fragmentation in its earliest forms: overwork, misplaced dependence, creeping burnout, compassion fatigue. With this awareness comes the chance to seek help—through prayer, confession, or clinical care—before we unravel further.

Second, living nephesh thrives in rhythm. In creation God established order: day and night, season and Sabbath. As image-bearers of the Breath-Giver, our lives are meant to reflect this cadence. Daily prayer. Regular sleep. Ordered meals. Movement balanced with rest. Faithfulness in taking prescribed medications. Sabbath stillness. These patterns do more than regulate us—they root us in the rhythms of God. When consistency fails, chaos creeps in. And where chaos reigns, fragmentation soon follows.

Finally, and most importantly, the living nephesh is directed toward its Source. In the Shema we are called to love God with all our heart, soul, and strength. Not only is this a call to integration, it is a call to orientation. Wholeness is not simply harmony within ourselves but alignment toward God. Wholeness sometimes means subtraction—saying no to what distracts or divides, saying no to toxic relationships, setting boundaries on work and technology, resisting what distracts or divides.

Instead, we reorient

- our hearts through worship, confession, and emotional honesty;

- our souls through prayer, fellowship, solitude, and silence;

- our strength through wise stewardship of time, energy, and financial resources.

In all of this, living nephesh is not a fixed state but a daily practice. One breath at a time. One choice at a time. One small act of alignment toward the Breath-Giver, who is ever ready to restore.

There are many real-life expressions of what it means to be a living nephesh. Among the most common—and most misunderstood—is how we care for our bodies, including through nutrition, movement, and medical care.

For many followers of Jesus, bodily disciplines can feel peripheral—or worse, vain. But in nephesh living, tending to the body is not vanity. It is fidelity.

When we nourish our bodies with intention, we honor the Breath-Giver, who filled them with life. When we move our bodies—through exercise, stretching, walking—we participate in the rhythms of life God designed for us. These actions are not divorced from our spiritual lives. They are expressions of it. Every healthy meal prepared with care, every walk taken to manage stress, every act of bodily stewardship becomes a kind of prayer—a quiet way of saying, "This life matters. This body matters. It belongs to God."

And this includes how we engage with medical care.

For many, the idea of taking medication—especially for mental health—carries stigma or shame. *If I had enough faith*, they think, *I wouldn't need this.* But the invitation to live nephesh reframes this entirely. Stewarding our health may very well include medication. Just as we would take antibiotics for an infection or insulin for diabetes, so too might we need antidepressants or mood stabilizers for chemical imbalances in the brain.

Medication compliance is not weakness. It is wisdom. It is love in action. It is faithfulness to the bodies we've been given.

As Paul reminds the Corinthians, our bodies are temples of the Holy Spirit (1 Corinthians 6:19). They are not ours to neglect or overmaster but are sacred spaces entrusted to our care.

EMBODIED PRAYER AND WORSHIP

When we tend to our bodies—through nourishment, through movement, through rest and prescribed care—we live as disciples, not in theory but in daily practice.

Boundaries, too, are a mark of the living soul.

To say no is not always resistance. Sometimes it is worship. No to late-night scrolling that heightens anxiety and disrupts rest. No to the overtime shift that would encroach on Sabbath space. No to conversations that erode instead of edify.

Proverbs 4:23 instructs us to guard our hearts, "for everything you do flows from it." In nephesh living we protect our wholeness not just through what we say yes to but through what we say no to. **Boundaries are not barriers—they are invitations to deeper presence**.

And if we are to live as living souls, we must also reimagine prayer and worship as more than words—expressions communicated in the choices, postures, and rhythms of daily life.

Prayer with our lips, yes, but also with our limbs. With our choices. With our posture and participation in the world.

To kneel beside our bed. To sing aloud while folding laundry. To journal our gratitude, our fears, our hopes. To light a candle, wash the dishes, breathe deeply, and give thanks—these too are prayers. These too are worship.

As Paul exhorts in Colossians 3:23–24, "Whatever you do, work at it with all your heart, as working for the Lord." In every motion of our day—whether mundane or monumental—we are offered the chance to commune with the Breath-Giver.

And finally, a living nephesh is not whole in isolation.

Small acts matter. Holding the door for a stranger. Listening without agenda. Writing a note of encouragement. Praying with your children. Laughing with a friend. Serving a neighbor.

These are not peripheral to our formation. They *are* formation. This is the Shema lived outward—wholeness poured into relationship. The restored soul becomes not just a private experience but a shared witness. As we love the Lord with all that we are, we inevitably begin to love others in kind.

This too is worship: the living soul offering itself—heart, soul, and strength—back to God, in the presence of others, for the good of the world.

THE DAILY INVITATION

Collectively, this is the invitation of the Shema. Of Jesus. Of living nephesh.

To live wholly, not perfectly.

To live fuller, not strive harder.

To walk with God in the midst of real life—school pickups, therapy sessions, fatigue, missed quiet times, morning jogs, laughter in the kitchen.

To offer every breath, every decision, every act of care as worship.

This is integration made real—Eden in the everyday.

It means we kneel not just in prayer but in presence.

We tithe with our money, our strength, and our very lives.

We trust not just our spirits to God but our bodies and minds too.

To live as a living nephesh is not to have all the pieces in place but to hand those pieces to the One who holds us together. The One who knit us in the womb. The One who breathes even now.

Yes, it's still messy.

But it's better.

Because God is mending.

So we live—not as those striving to assemble a perfect life but as those invited into a deeper reality.

A life rooted in the quiet confidence of being fully known and fully loved.

A life where every breath, every decision, every act of care becomes a living prayer.

Not because we have to. But because we are His.

This is the call of the living nephesh.
Presence, not perfection.
Abiding, not striving.
Becoming, not surviving.
A life whole and holy.
A life that is His.

Pause here.

Breathe in: *I am a living soul.*

Breathe out: *And I am being made whole.*

This life—your life—is not an accident. It is an altar.

Offer it fully. Live it fully.

REFLECTION: LIVING NEPHESH

- Where do you feel the strain of disintegration—where your mind, body, or spirit are out of sync?

- What rhythms help you live whole? What disrupts them?

- Are there boundaries you need to set, not out of fear but in faithfulness?

- What would it mean to offer your strength—your time, energy, or resources—as worship this week?

- Where might God be gently inviting you to breathe again, to begin again?

MAY THE SPIRIT DRAW YOU INTO THE FULLNESS OF LIFE—
WHERE HEART, MIND, BODY, AND SPIRIT ARE UNITED IN
MANIFEST LOVE FOR GOD.

6

DISCERNING DISINTEGRATION

Search me, God, and know my heart; test me and know my anxious thoughts.

PSALM 139:23

HE CAME IN FOR A ROUTINE FOLLOW-UP. A husband. A father. A business owner. A respected leader in his church—teaching Sunday school, coordinating mission trips. A paragon of excellence: brilliant, composed, generous, spiritually grounded, humble. His quiet confidence was always striking the moment I entered the room.

But today the air felt different. Thicker. Heavier.

"I don't feel like myself these days," he said quietly. Then almost reflexively, he sat up straighter, smoothing his tone. "I'm not in crisis," he clarified, "but I'm not well."

He told me God had been drawing his attention to what he described as a "glowing check engine light." He wasn't eating well.

Wasn't exercising. His sleep was scattered. His prayer life was still consistent, he said, but it felt flat—dry and unfulfilling.

He didn't use the word *depressed*, but the signs were there: emotional dullness, physical depletion, a growing sense of spiritual distance.

What troubled him most, though, was a thought he couldn't shake—one that his robust theology had always helped him guard against. But now it crept in uninvited: *Have I failed God? Or has He stepped away?*

He is not alone.

NAMING DISINTEGRATION

What he describes—fatigue without crisis, distance without rebellion, the quiet sense that something is off—is a kind of disintegration I see often, especially among those who appear outwardly "well." And for followers of Jesus, these seasons can be particularly disorienting. We know the practices. We believe the truth. And yet ... the wheels wobble. The soul that once felt unified—clear in purpose, anchored in worship, alive to God—drifts. Mind, body, and spirit lose their rhythm. The heart still believes, but it no longer burns.

This is not a new story. It's the long ache of the soul trying to return home. The living nephesh, made to live whole before God, loses its shape—not all at once—slowly, almost imperceptibly. Silently.

This chapter is about naming that drift.

It is about learning to discern when the living soul begins to fragment in quiet erosion. When the body signals exhaustion. When the mind numbs. When the prayers flatten. When the person who once lived whole becomes undone.

Not because they've failed.

Not because they lack faith.

But because they are human—living souls—and wholeness requires tending.

God's design for living nephesh is one of harmony: heart, soul, and strength working together in alignment with Him. But when these facets fall out of sync, disintegration follows. This fracture isn't new—it's inherited. In the fall humanity lost its original integration—with God and within itself. Through Jesus that alignment is restored. In Him we are reoriented to the Breath-Giver: heart awakened, soul quickened, strength restored.

Yet the battle is not over.

Even as redeemed souls, we live within a fractured world.

And in this world, drift is constant.

Disintegration rarely announces itself. It slips in through the cracks: persistent fatigue, dwindling motivation, emotional dullness, compulsive habits, spiritual numbness. These are not always dramatic or diagnostic; they often live between the lines—beneath the radar of screening tools, outside the standard classification of mental disorders—yet their weight is real. Mental health literature calls this "subthreshold" or "subclinical" distress: emotional and spiritual strain that doesn't meet formal thresholds for depression or anxiety but still disrupts a person's capacity to function, connect, and rest.[1] In clinical practice, these gray zones are significant—easy to overlook but deeply formative.

SPIRITUAL ENTROPY

The world presses into our fractures with constancy, not chaos.

It doesn't shatter the soul.

It wears it thin.

It doesn't come roaring like a storm.

It comes whispering day after day, quietly willing our souls into disintegration.

Left unchecked, entropy pulls our inner life toward disorder—slowly unraveling the once-integrated weave of heart, soul, and strength until

---

1   H. M. van Praag, E. R. de Kloet, et al., *Stress, the Brain and Depression* (Cambridge University Press, 2004), 3–5.

we no longer remember what wholeness feels like.

We live under the weight of a disorienting force, one that whispers that disconnection is normal, even admirable. The very traits that undermine our wholeness—overwork, performance, self-reliance—are often rewarded by the systems around us. And so it becomes possible to live a fully functioning external life while the internal world misfires. Outward success can mask inward disarray.

Sometimes it can even stand in opposition to the slow healing work God longs to do within.

This unraveling takes many forms.

One of the most ironic tensions is that its warning signs often masquerade as strength.

In clinic I often hear a familiar "Doing well. Staying busy."

It sounds benign. Harmless. Productive even.

But often it's a mask—a thin veil over a fractured soul.

Busyness becomes a culturally accepted form of self-medication—a relentless pace that drowns out the still, small voice of God. And in drowning out His voice, it disrupts His work. Because the soul is not restored by hustle. It is restored by presence.

> When busyness and perfectionism intertwine, they create a potent spiritual toxin. Left unchecked, they feed disintegration that often ends in burnout—not just physical or professional collapse but spiritual: a soul-level exhaustion that numbs the heart, detaches the will, and dims the light of joy.

Disintegration rarely wears the same face twice.

For the high-capacity leader, it shows up as quiet detachment: still showing up, still delivering, but without joy. Tasks once fueled by purpose now feel like burdens to survive.

For the devoted parent, it takes the form of silent depletion: pouring out for children, spouse, family but neglecting their own inner world. There is no time to breathe, no room to tend the soul beneath the surface.

For the perfectionist it emerges as brittle faith: devotions become checklists, prayers become performance, and the God of grace becomes like a distant supervisor.

These portraits are not meant to accuse but to awaken. Each reveals a soul longing for integration, a living nephesh waiting to be re-knit.

Another flashpoint comes in the realm of identity.

God created us to know ourselves first as His children—beloved, chosen, co-heirs with Christ. But in a world that prizes roles and production, it's easy to over-identify with what we do: parent, pastor, provider, performer. These are good callings, holy even, but they were never meant to bear the full weight of our identity.

When they do, when our worth becomes tethered to our output, disintegration sets in. We may still serve faithfully, still appear devoted, but inside, the compass shifts. Heart, soul, and strength are no longer oriented toward God. They bend toward the approval of others, the illusion of control, the fear of falling short.

And so we drift.

Still showing up.

Still functioning.

But no longer whole.

THE SILENT SHAME OF THE FAITHFUL

Throughout my career God has pressed me to attend closely to the seasons of the human soul. Family medicine allows this like few other vocations—births, graduations, diagnoses, recoveries, marriages, retirements, deaths. Often within the same family. Sometimes within the same person.

As a young physician and follower of Jesus, I once assumed that Christians—armed with Scripture's promises—would weather these seasons with more resilience. Surely we who know we are never alone, who trust in a Savior who has suffered, who cling to the hope of resurrection, would walk through hardship differently.

Yet over the years, I've witnessed something profoundly human—and quietly heartbreaking: Christians often suffer more when they feel spiritually disoriented.

Not because they lack faith but because they feel ashamed for needing it.

Instead of receiving their weariness as an invitation, they see it as a failure.

As if faith should render them immune to exhaustion, doubt, or grief.

But here is the truth: deep faith does not preclude deep weariness.

Jesus wept.

He grew angry.

He felt the sting of betrayal, the ache of loss, the agony of separation.

In Him, we are invited to bring our full humanity before God—not just the strong parts but the trembling, uncertain ones.

And when we do, we are met not with rebuke but with recognition.

El Roi.

The God who sees.

The psalms give us this language of honest lament.

Psalm 42 aches with longing: "Why, my soul [nephesh], are you downcast? Why so disturbed within me?" (v. 5).

The psalmist remembers past joy but feels far from it in the present.

He doesn't rush to resolve the tension. Instead, he holds it. "My tears have been my food day and night.... I will yet praise him" (vv. 3, 5).

Psalm 88 goes even deeper into the valley. There is no tidy ending. No uplifting refrain. Only raw, unfiltered despair: "Darkness is my closest friend" (v. 18).

And yet this too is prayer. This too is Scripture.

Jesus Himself also entered the landscape of disintegration.

In Gethsemane He confessed to His friends, "My soul is overwhelmed with sorrow to the point of death" (Mark 14:34). On the cross He cried the raw words of Psalm 22: "My God, my God, why have you forsaken me?" (v. 1).

He knew exhaustion. Isolation. The ache of feeling abandoned.

Yet in Him, fragmentation was not the end of the story. Through His death and resurrection, the shattering of the human condition became the doorway to restoration. His wounds are not erased; they are glorified. His risen body bears the marks of redemption—a promise that what is fractured can be made whole.

These Scriptures teach us something sacred:

To *feel* lost is not to *be* lost. To feel disintegrated is not to be disqualified.

These cries are not signs of spiritual failure but invitations to come near.

Disorientation, then, is not the enemy of faith.

It is often its doorway.

A summons to pause. To listen. To let the fractured soul speak its truth before the One who can hold it all.

This is how healing begins: by naming our fragmentation, not denying it.

By falling into the arms of a God who makes us whole, not by simply pushing through.

And yet even as Scripture gives us language for this ache, modern clinical tools often struggle to name it. This is where the limitations of our diagnostic systems become clear.

WHAT THE DSM MISSES

There is a difference between a diagnosis and a soul that is disintegrating.

In clinical practice we are trained to recognize patterns. Depression. Anxiety. Adjustment disorder. Each with its criteria, thresholds, and time courses. These categories are essential—they provide clarity, consistency, and access to care. But they also have limits.

Because the soul rarely speaks in checklists.

What many patients describe—a kind of subtle unraveling; a fatigue that's not just physical; a loss of presence, meaning, or purpose—often lives between the lines of diagnostic criteria, or the DSM (*Diagnostic and Statistical Manual of Mental Disorders*). It doesn't always meet the threshold for major depression. It may not present as panic attacks or insomnia.

But it is real. And if left unnamed, it quietly deepens.

As clinicians we can feel this gap. We hear the sigh at the end of the sentence. We see the weight in their shoulders. We know something isn't right. But it doesn't quite "code."

Discernment, in this light, is not just a spiritual practice. It's a clinical necessity too. It's how we love our patients—and ourselves—well, even when the data is inconclusive but the soul is crying out.

This is where discernment becomes a vital tool—especially for those who follow Jesus.

Because fragmentation of the soul is not always a disorder. It's often a sign.

A sign that something has gone off course. That the person before us—though still functioning—is no longer whole. Their heart, soul, and strength are not aligned. The rhythms that once sustained them have broken down. And more than a diagnosis, they need a name for what they're experiencing. They need space to tell the truth.

To say, "I'm not okay."

To ask, "What's happening to me?"

To hear, "You're not crazy. You're not weak. You're being invited."

An invitation to slow down.

To reflect.

To name what's been lost.

To listen for what the Spirit might be whispering beneath the surface.

DISCERNING FROM WITHIN

Thankfully, the work of recognizing inner disintegration is not ours to bear alone. The Spirit—named by Jesus as both *Helper* and *Advocate*—beckons us to attend to the places within us that cry out for healing. Discernment, in this sense, is not judgment. It is realignment. The gentle tuning of the living soul.

While discernment is ultimately a gift from the Spirit, we can cooperate with His work by cultivating practices that make us more pliable, more open to His guidance.

Silence is essential. In the rush of modern life, we are immersed in a rising tide of noise and distraction. But to hear the voice of God—especially when He is gently naming our hidden fractures—we must create space. It is often in the quiet that we become aware of the subtle dissonance within us.

Practically, this may begin with five unhurried minutes in the morning, sitting with a Psalm. The psalms were the songbook of Jesus—He prayed them, quoted them, leaned on them throughout His life. We too are invited to soak in their language, not rushing through but lingering. Sitting with Scripture, savoring the words without agenda, praying them in the way Jesus did.

Prayer is presence. In seasons of disintegration, prayer is more than intercession or petition. It is not a performance or a ritual to "fix" ourselves. It is the practice of being with God—honest, raw, unguarded. It's not about perfect words but about bringing our whole, fragmented selves into His presence. This might mean whispered prayers of "Here I am, Lord" or simply sitting in silence before Him, trusting that He sees, hears, and welcomes us as we are. In prayer, we practice the very presence we long to rediscover—abiding in the Breath-Giver who restores us.

The prayer of examen, an ancient spiritual practice, helps us take this a step further. By slowing down to reflect on the events of the day, we examine our responses, notice what stirred or unsettled us, and look with gratitude for God's presence in it all. This daily rhythm helps us become more attuned to both our fragmentation and God's faithful nearness.

This may be fully unpacked, as it is in the "Reflection" section of this chapter—or it may take a simpler, more condensed form. Two evening questions can carry surprising power: Where did I feel close to God today? Where did I resist Him?

Over time this practice sharpens our awareness of drift and draws us gently back to center.

Journaling reorients us. Journaling is another powerful companion in discernment—for lament and for gratitude. As we write, we engage in a holy act of noticing. And this noticing transforms us. The spiritual practice of recording God's goodness echoes a profound neurological reality: Over time intentional reflection activates the brain's capacity for neuroplasticity—the ability to rewire and reshape itself—forming us into people who see with grace and gratitude.[2]

This need not be eloquent or even written in a formal journal. Sometimes it's just a few lines on a scrap of paper:

What I'm grateful for today.

Where I need help.

Practicing gratitude daily shapes us into people who carry it instinctively.

Community plays a vital role. "Faithful are the wounds of a friend," Proverbs reminds us (Proverbs 27:6 ESV).

Trusted spiritual companions—people who love us, speak truth, and walk alongside us—often see what we cannot. Living nephesh is never a solitary journey. As image-bearers of a triune God, we are made for mutual presence. When we live vulnerably in the presence of others, their perspective becomes a mirror through which the Spirit can speak.

This is the soil where discernment often blossoms: A trusted friend. A quiet confession. A willingness to be seen.

These open the soul to correction and to the comfort we cannot

---

2   "The Neuroscience of Gratitude: How Being Thankful Rewires Your Brain," Integrity Psychological Services, accessed October 30, 2025.

summon on our own. Transparent, vulnerable community—especially when led by those with a bleed-first humility—paves the way for two of the most powerful, transformative words we can hear: "Me too."

Recognizing that we are not alone in our struggles is often where healing begins.

Psalm 139:23–24 offers a final, powerful posture of discernment: "Search me, God, and know my heart; test me and know my anxious thoughts. See if there is any offensive way in me, and lead me in the way everlasting."

In the end, discerning disintegration is not a call to hypervigilance or self-criticism. It is an invitation.

An invitation to notice—to pay attention to the small signals, the quiet longings, the places of unrest within.

An invitation to yield—to lay those places before God without shame or defense, trusting that what feels like failure is often the starting point of grace.

And an invitation to be restored by the gentle work of the Spirit, who brings wholeness where we have frayed—not by our striving.

This is the movement of living nephesh.

Pause here.

Take this moment as an invitation, not a task. The ancient practice of the examen offers us a way to gently trace the shape of our days, to notice where God has been near, and to discern where our soul is asking to be restored.

Breathe in: *Search me, God.*

Breathe out: *Heal my soul.*

REFLECTION: A GUIDED EXAMEN FOR THE LIVING SOUL

Find a quiet place. Breathe deeply. Ask the Spirit to guide you. Then slowly walk through these steps:[3]

1. GRATITUDE

    Look back over your day or week. Where did you sense God's goodness? Where did beauty, love, or joy brush up against you? Pause to give thanks.

2. PRESENCE

    Where were you most alive? Where were you most drained? Notice without judgment. What moments drew your heart toward God? What moments pulled you away?

3. ATTENTION

    When did you sense disconnection—from God, yourself, or others? Were there moments of drift, fatigue, anger, numbness? Gently name them.

---

3   If you'd like to take this further—exploring specific signs of spiritual and emotional drift in your own life—appendix A offers a simple inventory. It's not a test but a mirror. A way to name what's surfaced and gently discern where the Spirit may be inviting restoration. You may choose to use it now or return to it later—during a retreat, a season of burnout, or any time your nephesh feels scattered.

4. CONFESSION AND RELEASE

Where do you need grace? Offer your failures, frustrations, or heaviness to God. Ask for the courage to release what no longer serves your wholeness.

5. INVITATION

Where is God inviting you into restoration? What rhythms, boundaries, or practices might help you live more fully as a living nephesh? Listen for a simple next step.

MAY THE BREATH-GIVER SEARCH YOUR SOUL WITH TENDERNESS, NAMING THE PLACES THAT ARE FRAYED, THAT YOU MIGHT DISCOVER THE WAY OF WHOLENESS AGAIN.

7

PRACTICING WHOLENESS

Do not despise these small beginnings, for the LORD rejoices to see the work begin.

ZECHARIAH 4:10 NLT

HE SAT ACROSS FROM ME, crisp white coat folded neatly in the corner of the room, stethoscope dangling from the pocket, shoulders slightly hunched. A physician. A colleague. A man whose résumé quietly announced excellence: board certified, published, respected, admired.

"I know what to tell them," he said quietly. "I just don't know how to live it myself."

He wasn't there for a formal visit—not really. He was a colleague, a friend, ducking into the office at the end of the day, seeking something he couldn't quite name.

He knew the guidelines: Exercise five days a week. Prioritize sleep. Eat whole foods. Pray, rest, connect, unplug. He could recite the recommendations in his sleep. But living them?

That was another matter.

"I've been reading about life coaching," he admitted with a half smile, "or maybe a personal trainer, or a dietitian ... just someone to help me figure out how to actually do the things I tell other people to do. Because right now it feels like I'm living in two worlds."

He didn't need more information.

What he needed was grace.

A place to begin.

Not a program. Not a ninety-day overhaul.

Just the first small step.

And that's the paradox of practicing wholeness: It is not about mastering everything at once. It's about beginning, gently and humbly, again and again.

AN INVITATION INTO PRACTICE

Chapter 6 helped us listen. But listening was never meant to leave us standing still.

Discernment opens the door to practice. It does not simply reveal where we are fractured. It shows us where we are invited to begin again.

The examen, the quiet inventory, the naming of drift—these were never meant as ends in themselves. They prepare us to step back into rhythm, to carry the small acts of grace that draw the soul toward home.

What does it mean to practice wholeness?

It means returning to life in step with the Spirit, living fully human, loving God with all our heart, soul, and strength—restored to Edenic unity. It is a movement toward integration: unity within ourselves and harmony with the world around us.

It is a return to walking with God in the cool of the day.

The most freeing part of this invitation is that it's universal. Integration of body and soul, mind and heart, self and neighbor—this is God's gift, freely given. But it is also a gift that invites our participation.

We are called to participate with God, not to perfect ourselves. The Spirit—our Helper, our Advocate—responds to even the smallest acts of devotion.

As the vignette reminds us, possessing knowledge does not guarantee the ability to live it. This tension is familiar to many of us, no matter our background. Often we stand at the edge of change feeling overwhelmed. We know what would bring health and wholeness—exercise, nourishing meals, spiritual practices—but we are paralyzed. The mountain feels too high, the journey too long. And so we stay where we are.

Many would refer to this phenomenon as *motivational inertia*. A body in motion tends to stay in motion. Healthy practices—whether physical, emotional, or spiritual—become self-sustaining over time. But like a boulder at rest, a life at rest tends to remain at rest. It often takes an extraordinary nudge to set things into motion.

There are intellectual barriers too. Many of us, especially those shaped by achievement culture, imagine wholeness as an all-or-nothing overhaul. "I need to fix everything." But this mindset often unravels, giving way to discouragement.

Overhaul often leads to overwhelm.

The invitation of living nephesh is gentler. It is gradual, kind, and paradoxically powerful.

Jesus described the kingdom of God as a farmer scattering seed.

He said, "This is what the kingdom of God is like. A man scatters seed on the ground. Night and day, whether he sleeps or gets up, the seed sprouts and grows, though he does not know how. All by itself the soil produces grain—first the stalk, then the head, then the full kernel in the head. As soon as the grain is ripe, he puts the sickle to it, because the harvest has come." (Mark 4:26–29)

Night and day the farmer goes about his life, and the seed sprouts and grows—though he knows not how.

Transformation unfolds quietly, almost imperceptibly, until one day it bears fruit.

Paul picks up this same image when he speaks of the "fruit of the

Spirit" (Galatians 5:22–23). He does not describe it as a product, a task, or an achievement, but as fruit—implying something organic, something that cannot be forced or rushed. As Tim Keller has often observed, fruit grows slowly, so slowly that you rarely notice it day to day.[1] But over seasons, over years, the change becomes unmistakable. What once seemed imperceptible becomes undeniable.

And so it is with wholeness.

The movement toward integration does not happen through drastic change. It happens through small, faithful steps. Through intentional rhythms. Through imperfect practices.

And over time they become transformative.

It is important to recognize that God doesn't merely promise us an end goal—glorification. He promises us a process: sanctification. A journey in which, day by day, we are formed more deeply into His likeness, becoming the person He created us to be. In the language of the early church, this transformation is called *theosis*—becoming by grace what God is by nature. It is the quiet, steady work of being drawn into God's life, not merely conformed outwardly but transformed inwardly into His love.

In a culture defined by performance and outcomes, we are profoundly conditioned to fix our eyes on the end result. But God gently challenges this instinct. What if the process itself is the gift? What if the journey between Eden and eternity is where His grace meets us most tenderly?

God calls us to faithfulness to the journey.

And He invites us to walk in a posture of trust and fidelity—not anxiety, not self-condemnation. The movement toward wholeness is Spirit led, not self-engineered. Our role is to participate in the process, not perfect it. God's invitation has always been this: to be faithful, not flawless.

---

1   Tim Keller notes this in particular in Timothy Keller, *Galatians for You* (Good Book Company, 2012).

THE GRACE OF SMALL STEPS

This changes how we begin.

Instead of rushing toward sweeping reform, we are invited into small, intentional steps. These are more than self-improvement practices. They are acts of integration: body, mind, and spirit brought into shared devotion.

In nephesh living, the physical carries spiritual meaning, and the spiritual is lived through the body. A walk taken in silence becomes a prayer. A meal prepared in gratitude becomes an offering laid upon the altar. A conversation offered in love becomes an act of worship. A run through the neighborhood becomes a liturgy of breath and movement. Washing dishes alongside a spouse becomes an offering of service. Rocking a restless child at 2:00 a.m. becomes a holy act of comfort, a gentle reminder of our Father's love for us.

These are not separate domains. They are the integrated life of the living soul.

What we learn through discernment practices like the examen becomes the compass for response. If examen reveals restlessness, we may be called to Sabbath rest. If it reveals anger, perhaps forgiveness practices or reconciliation. If it shows overextension, simplicity and margin become disciplines of faithfulness. If it uncovers ungratefulness, a daily gratitude prayer or journal may anchor us back to God. These are not generic spiritual tasks—they are integrated responses, tethering heart, mind, body, and strength into worship.

And as we do, we discover what Jesus meant when He spoke of the easy yoke, the light burden. We realize the Spirit is not demanding perfection. He is inviting presence.

Here, we establish core rhythms—practical, intentional patterns of life designed to heal the disintegration of the nephesh and reorient us toward the heartbeat of our Father. These rhythms are Spirit-led movements, not mechanical habits or self-improvement projects: the Spirit illuminating our broken places and then gently guiding us toward healing and reintegration.

Though these rhythms take many forms, they are not separate compartments or checkboxes. As we recover from the wounds of dualism, we remind ourselves—speaking to our very nephesh, as the psalmist often did—that the physical and spiritual are deeply intertwined.

The Spirit may nudge us toward care of the body.

We might begin with breath-and-body rhythms:

- MOVEMENT AS WORSHIP—walking, stretching, even mundane tasks like folding laundry or mowing the lawn, approached with gratitude for the everyday mercies of strength and motion, even in the mundane.

- REST AS RESISTANCE—sleep, Sabbath, and bodily restoration as acts of trust in God's provision, defying a culture that never stops.

- BREATH PRAYERS—aligning our breath with the Breath-Giver, letting each inhale and exhale draw us back to God.

If the Spirit exposes restlessness of mind or spiritual stagnancy, we turn toward the life of the mind and attention.

- SCRIPTURE MEDITATION—not for information but for slow, prayerful rumination.

- PRAYING THE PSALMS, reading them as blessings over ourselves.

- LECTIO DIVINA, OR INDUCTIVE STUDY—approaching Scripture with openness and curiosity.

- DAILY EXAMEN OR REFLECTION—Where was God present today? Where did we resist? Where are we being invited deeper?

- SIMPLICITY AND MARGIN—making space to attend to what matters.

If the Spirit highlights relational strain or loneliness, we cultivate presence with others.

- INTENTIONAL CONNECTION—shared meals, unhurried time with family or friends, conversation that matters.

- VULNERABILITY IN COMMUNITY—allowing trusted companions to see us, know us, and speak truth into our lives.

- ACTS OF SERVICE—small ways to love our neighbor and reflect God's care.

If burnout has taken hold, we return to rest and delight.

- SABBATH KEEPING—echoing the eternal cadence of God; delighting in rest, gratitude, and holy nonproductivity.

- CREATIVE PRACTICES—art, music, writing, gardening, cooking—tending the soul through beauty, awakening the creative breath (*ruach*) God placed within us.

- CELEBRATION AND GRATITUDE—marking joy, even small joy, as an echo of God's goodness.

When we integrate these small graces into our lives—not perfectly but patiently, consistently—we experience reintegration within ourselves and with God.

And we remember the paradox of the Spirit's work:

Small is faithful.

Imperfect can still be holy.

Rhythms are not rules; they are lifelines.

THE PRACTICE OF RETURNING

Recognizing and anticipating the barriers to these life-giving rhythms is essential if we are to avoid discouragement or the slow erosion of momentum. These are not questions of *if*, but *when*. Our own weaknesses, biases, and stories—shaped by family, culture, and old wounds—will inevitably tug at us, drawing us back toward disintegration, toward spiritual entropy. Perfectionism, shame, all-or-nothing thinking, the fear of failing again—these are only a few of the pitfalls along the way.

But here is the invitation: to reimagine how we understand failure.

Failure is not merely inevitable on the path of spiritual formation; it is essential. Practicing wholeness—inhabiting the fullness of our created selves—is not about flawless execution or uninterrupted progress. It is about returning.

In Scripture this sacred act of turning—again and again—is called *repentance*. Not shame, not penance, but return. The soul remembering where it belongs and choosing, even haltingly, to go back.

This journey is not measured by achievement but by presence.

And here is the truth we must hold close: The act of returning is itself an act of wholeness. Every time we turn back to God, every time we take even a small step toward reintegration, we declare what Adam and Eve could not yet see—that God is not waiting to cast us out but to restore us. He beckons us home again and again, to heal our souls.

And so we are left with this simple invitation: In the landscape of your own life, where might you practice wholeness this week?

One place. One step. One beginning.

Keep it small. Keep it grace filled.

Perhaps it's a breath of stillness in the midst of hurry.

Perhaps it's attending to your body with kindness.

Perhaps it's tending to a relationship that has been waiting for your presence.

If it helps, write it down. Share it with a friend. Offer it quietly to God in prayer.

Let it be not a project to complete but an act of returning.

A reminder that you were never meant to live in pieces.

Wholeness begins in presence rather than mastery—one quiet step, one surrendered breath at a time.

As you take even one small step toward practicing wholeness, remember this: You are already a living nephesh—whole, beloved, formed by God's hands, animated by His breath, sustained by His love.

Practicing wholeness is not about earning something you lack. It is about living what is already true—returning to the wholeness of who you are, who you have always been, who you are being remade to become.

> Every small act of alignment, every quiet moment of return, every breath offered in surrender—none of it is insignificant. It is all part of God's mending work in you.

Wholeness is not a finish line to cross. It is a lifelong practice: of presence, of becoming, of allowing God to restore you again and again.

So as you rise, as you move into the ordinary and sacred spaces of your life, carry this truth: You are being made whole.

And God, the Breath-Giver, goes with you.

NEPHESH LIVING

Pause here.

Breathe in: *Bless these steps, Lord.*

Breathe out: *Make them faithful.*

Start where you are.

One step. One breath. One grace.

And let each one carry you home.

REFLECTION: PRACTICING PRESENCE

Wholeness is not a project to complete or a finish line to reach. It is a practice of returning.

- Where in your life have you felt the pull toward disintegration?

- Where have you noticed fragmentation in your body, your relationships, your rhythms, or your sense of God? Take a moment to name just one place.

- What would it look like this week to take a small step toward returning—not to mastery but to presence?

Consider writing this intention down.

Share it with a friend or mentor.

Offer it to God as an act of trust, believing that even the smallest return matters.[2]

REMEMBER–YOU ARE NOT BEGINNING FROM ABSENCE.

YOU ARE BEGINNING FROM THE PRESENCE OF GOD ALREADY

AT WORK IN YOU.

---

2   If you'd like help imagining what that small step could look like, turn to appendix B. It offers a simple, grace-filled collection of practical ways to practice wholeness—organized around the core rhythms of breath, body, belonging, becoming, and blessing. These are not rules or checklists but invitations—small, sustainable practices you can return to again and again as you live into the wholeness God has already begun in you.

8

RULES OF LIFE FOR THE
LIVING SOUL

Abide in me, and I in you. As the branch cannot bear fruit by itself, unless it abides in the vine, neither can you, unless you abide in me.

JOHN 15:4-5 ESV

SHE CAME IN FOR HER ANNUAL VISIT, the first time in years without a crisis pulling her through the door.

Type 2 diabetes, hypertension, a long history of anxiety—all written in the chart. But today her blood pressure was steady, her A1c down, her eyes clearer. She sat with a kind of settledness I hadn't seen before.

"I've been walking most mornings," she told me, "just around the neighborhood. Not far, but enough to feel the air on my face."

She laughed softly. "I even started cooking again. Nothing fancy—some vegetables, some soup. I try to eat sitting down now."

She spoke of small things with quiet weight: setting her phone down in the evenings, meeting with her Divorce Care group at church every

Wednesday night, leaving space in her day to rest without apology.

"It's not much," she said, almost apologetically. "But it's keeping me steady."

What struck me wasn't just the labs or the practices. It was the way she occupied the room. Her breathing was slower. Her speech less rushed. She met my eyes without the flicker of distraction or defeat I remembered from earlier visits.

When we discussed her next steps—medications, labs, follow-ups—she nodded, not out of resignation or compliance but out of something quieter: trust.

She was living with a kind of rhythm. Not perfectly, not without setbacks, but faithfully. And it was bearing fruit.

CULTIVATING RHYTHMS OF WHOLENESS

This is what a rule of life looks like in the real world.

Not a checklist. Not a program. Not a flawless performance.

A rule of life is a quiet rhythm of abiding—the kind Jesus speaks of in John 15—where small, deliberate choices create space for life to take root. We aren't meant to bear fruit by force of will. We are meant to stay connected to the Source.

To abide is to remain. To live close. To grow in rhythm with God's life rather than striving to sustain our own apart from Him. A rule of life simply helps us tend to that connection. It gathers the scattered pieces of our lives—breath and body, work and rest, solitude and community—and teaches us how to carry them as one integrated offering before God.

A rule of life doesn't earn love or favor.

It helps us practice living in the love already given.

A rule of life is less a list of tasks than a trellis—humble supports for life to grow.

The word *rule* traces back to the Latin *regula*—not just "rule" but "straight rod" or measuring stick.[1] A guide. A humble framework. A set of simple, flexible supports—practices, rhythms, postures—onto which we entrust our small, daily decisions.

We do not abide by willpower alone. We abide by arranging our lives so that abiding becomes possible.

The trellis does not create fruit; it simply lifts the vine, giving it space to flourish.

This is what a rule of life offers: a framework that steadies us in love, shapes us without suffocation, and makes room for slow, hidden fruitfulness. We do not build trellises to control growth.

We build them to support it.

AN ANCIENT FRAMEWORK FOR WHOLENESS

A rule of life isn't an optional layer of devotion.

It is the quiet work of integration.

For the living nephesh, this matters deeply.

We are not just bodies. Not just souls. Not merely thoughts, feelings, or roles. We are whole beings—physical, relational, emotional, spiritual—designed to live as one.

A rule of life helps us resist what pulls us apart. In a world of hurry, anxiety, and disconnection, it calls us back—to presence, to attention, to love. And it's not about doing more. It's about aligning with what already matters most.

This is far from a modern innovation.

Scripture has long imagined a life ordered toward love and wholeness.

"Abide in me, and I in you."

Sabbath woven into creation.

The Shema recited morning and night.

---

1   *Merriam-Webster*, "rule," accessed November 3, 2025, https://unabridged.merriam-webster.com/collegiate/rule.

The quiet kingdom growing like seed, hidden but sure.

A rule of life helps us remember these patterns: The point was never perfection but faithful practice.

This is the invitation of Jesus. His words are precise and tender: "I am the vine; you are the branches" (John 15:5 ESV).

He is the source—verdant, rooted, alive.

We are the ones invited to remain. To stay. To abide.

ABIDING: But Jesus makes clear in John 15 that abiding is an active rhythm. A discipline. The Greek word *meno* means "to remain," "to continue," "to make one's home." Abiding is a conscious return, not a static state. A rule of life helps us live this return, especially in seasons of drought or storm. It holds us close to the source, even when the fruit is still unseen.

THE SABBATH: Genesis 2 gives us a cadence written into the cosmos: God worked—and then God rested. Not from exhaustion but for delight.

Rest was always to be a gift, not a recovery plan.

As Jesus later reminded us, "The Sabbath was made for man [humanity], not man [humanity] for the Sabbath" (Mark 2:7). The Breath-Giver invites us to stop. To delight. To remember: We are not machines. We are living souls, sustained by His breath.

THE SHEMA: "You shall love the Lord your God with all your heart, soul, and strength."

In the Shema, the word translated as "soul," *nephesh*, is a reminder that the love of God is meant to be lived with our whole integrated being. For generations this verse gave shape to ordinary days—spoken morning and evening, along the road, at the table, in the rhythm of life.

It was never intended as abstract belief. It was a pattern, a lived response of love woven through time.

THE QUIET KINGDOM: Jesus said the kingdom is like seed scattered on the ground. It sprouts and grows, though the farmer doesn't fully know how. Mystery is part of the design. Grace is revealed in the slow unfolding.

We are to tend the ground, resisting the urge to explain or control the harvest.

These ancient patterns—abiding, resting, loving, tending—are not burdens.

They are invitations to return to the life we were made for.

And they are always relational, not transactional. These patterns do not earn love; they help us dwell in the love already given.

To live as whole souls, fully present with God and with others.

FIVE ANCHORING MOVEMENTS

How do we begin to embody these ancient patterns today? How do we move from longing to practice, from good intentions to graceful rhythms?

These five dimensions of wholeness form a simple trellis:

Breath.

Body.

Belonging.

Becoming.

Blessing.

Each one offers a space for abiding amid the ordinary.

BREATH: CREATING SPACE TO RECEIVE. Breath draws us back to the One who sustains.

It is the pause that breaks the tyranny of the urgent,

the stillness that makes room for God's voice,

the rest that reminds us we are not held up by our own striving.

A rule of life centered on breath moves us beyond occasional moments of quiet into rhythms that shape the flow of our days, weeks, and seasons.

This may look like:

- A set time for morning or evening prayer—steady, even when the heart feels empty or distracted.

- A weekly Sabbath—a day not of achievement but of ceasing, delighting, resting, and worshipping.

- A commitment to daily margin—protecting time from the pull of productivity, leaving an hour unscheduled for breath, wonder, and God.

These are ways of remembering that abiding love is not something we chase or earn; it is something we receive.

And to receive, we must slow.

BODY: PRACTICES OF MOVEMENT, NOURISHMENT, AND CARE. To tend to the body is not to step away from the spiritual life but to step more fully into it.

For many of us, the body has been a place of quiet tension—pushed too hard, ignored too long, or treated as a machine to be optimized.

A rule of life for the body invites us to remember that this body is part of our worship, part of how we love God with all that we are.

Practices may include:

- A daily walk—a rhythm of presence and renewal, not measured by performance.

- A weekly practice of mindful meals—attentive to what we eat but also how we eat, turning nourishment into prayer.

- A commitment to rest—setting limits around sleep, honoring fatigue as part of tending to faith.

- A rhythm of medical care—attending to the body's needs with consistency as an act of stewardship and grace, not just in times of crisis.

These are not scattered acts of self-improvement. They are a framework of love—a quiet, repeated way of saying with our bodies:

We are God's, and we are loved.

BELONGING: PRACTICES OF RELATIONSHIP, VULNERABILITY, AND COMMUNITY. We don't become whole in isolation. We are shaped, held, and healed in the presence of others—

in laughter and grief, in confession and forgiveness,

in shared tables and long conversations and quiet acts of care.

A rule of life around belonging calls us to move beyond accidental connection into intentional patterns of relationship. It invites us to tether our lives to others, to practice presence, vulnerability, and faithful love over time.

You might practice this by:

- A commitment to a small group or faith community—where you are known by name, and your absence is felt.

- A rhythm of shared meals—a steady practice of hospitality and welcome, not just for holidays and celebrations.

- A practice of reconciliation—reaching out to repair what is broken, becoming a peacemaker instead of drifting away.

These are not mere social gestures. They are acts of love, resistance against loneliness, and practices of living as whole souls within the body of Christ.

BECOMING: PRACTICES OF GROWTH, LEARNING, VOCATION, AND CREATIVITY. We are always being shaped.

Never static, never finished, never beyond the reach of God's transforming love.

To abide as a living soul is to live open to becoming—not toward perfection but toward deeper love, freedom, and wholeness.

A rule of life around becoming invites us to lean into growth with intention, to create patterns that stretch us beyond comfort and awaken us to God's work within and around us.

Consider:

- A rhythm of learning—committing to read, study, or reflect in ways that nourish your heart and mind.

- A practice of creativity—setting aside time to write, paint, garden, build, or play—for delight, not achievement.

- A rule of vocation—offering gifts in steady, faithful service at work, church, or in the neighborhood, participating in God's renewing work.

These are not projects of self-improvement. They are quiet yeses to God's transforming love, forming us anew.

BLESSING: EXTENDING DIGNITY, GENEROSITY, AND LOVE TOWARD OTHERS AS AN INTENTIONAL OUTFLOW OF WHOLENESS. We are not made whole for ourselves alone.

We are made to become channels of blessing—extending love, dignity, and care to the world around us.

Blessing is how our wholeness turns outward, how God's love moves through us to touch others.

A rule of life for blessing invites us to live missionally—through small, consistent, faithful acts of love and justice, not only through occasional grand gestures.

Ways to live this out might include:

- A rhythm of hospitality—opening your table to friends, neighbors, strangers.

- A practice of generosity—offering income, time, or energy to support justice and mercy.

- A rule of presence—training your gaze to see others as sacred, offering kindness and care to the overlooked.

These are not spiritual add-ons. They are the fruit of wholeness—quiet, daily witnesses that proclaim:

You matter.

Your body matters.

Your life is sacred.

Blessing reminds us that wholeness is given to be shared, a participation in God's healing of the world.

These five spheres do not stand alone. They interlace. Breath opens space for belonging. Caring for the body creates capacity for becoming. Blessing flows from the overflow of the others.

As we tend one, the Spirit often stirs movement across them all—drawing us into an integrated life in which no part is isolated and every part is held in grace.

This is the heart of living nephesh: a life where breath, body, relationship, growth, and love intertwine as one whole offering before God.

These five anchors provide a comprehensive, though by no means exhaustive, framework for living as a whole soul. They serve as a memorable guide, helping us shape rules of life that are spacious, integrative, and grace filled.

CRAFTING YOUR OWN RULE OF LIFE

This chapter unfolds as a gentle progression alongside the previous two: First, helping us awaken to the places of disintegration within. Then inviting us into gentle, Spirit-led steps toward healing. And finally, offering trellises—simple frameworks—on which those small steps can grow into enduring, transformative pathways of life with God.

But these frameworks are not prescriptive or rigid.

A rule of life is deeply personal, shaped by season, calling, and the Spirit's unique work in each of us.

As you begin crafting your own, a few gentle guidelines may help:

- KEEP IT SIMPLE. Start small. Choose practices that create space, not strain.

- KEEP IT GRACE FILLED. This is about presence with God, not the pursuit of perfection.

- REVISIT OVER TIME. Your rule is a living framework, not a fixed contract. Let it shift as seasons change.

- HONOR YOUR CURRENT SEASON. Shape a rule that fits where you are now.

- BEGIN SMALL. Choose one area—breath, belonging, body.

- EXPERIMENT AND STAY CURIOUS. Notice what gives life.

- RESIST PERFECTIONISM. This is your journey, not anyone else's.

- AVOID MAKING IT A SELF-IMPROVEMENT PROJECT. You are a beloved soul to be tended.

- FOCUS ON ALIGNMENT, NOT ACHIEVEMENT. The fruit is not in flawless execution but in quiet returning.

Think of your rule of life as one living trellis, not five separate tracks—a single, grace-shaped framework that supports the whole of who you are—bringing body and soul back into integrated nephesh living.

Each small practice is not its own rule.

Each is a strand, woven together to help you live as a whole soul before God.

A beginning example might be:

- BREATH: Five minutes of prayerful silence before the noise of the day.

- BODY: A short evening walk, not for fitness but for exhale.

- BELONGING: A weekly meal with someone who knows your name and your story.

- BECOMING: Reading one spiritually formative book over the next few months.

- BLESSING: A phone call weekly to someone the Spirit places on your heart.

These are not checkboxes or spiritual achievements.

They are gentle anchors—quiet ways of saying *this part of me matters too*.

Remember, you're not building a perfect life.

You're learning how to carry your soul—whole—before God.

Crafting a rule of life means tending the whole of who you are, rather than managing scattered parts. It is an act of love for the living nephesh—a way of aligning our days, our desires, our movements with God's presence and purpose.

In appendix C you'll find space to begin shaping your own rule of life—a simple, integrative framework rooted in breath, body, belonging, becoming, and blessing. It isn't a template to perfect—it's a place to listen, respond, and shape a rhythm that fits your season.

In the end, crafting a rule of life is not a call to master our days or perfect our practices.

It is an invitation.

To return.

To align.

To abide.

Pause here.

Breathe in: *You are the vine, Lord.*

Breathe out: *Help me to abide.*

A rule of life is a trellis—a simple framework to hold your soul steady

Choose practices that create space for God's life to flow.

Choose what steadies you.

Practice it with grace.

Abide and bear fruit.

REFLECTION: CRAFTING A RULE OF LIFE

Take a quiet moment. Breathe deeply. Let your whole self come to rest in God's presence. As you reflect, begin listening for the shape of your own rule of life—not as a perfect plan but as a living framework, cultivated in grace.

- Where in my life do I sense integration—where breath, body, belonging, becoming, and blessing flow together in wholeness?

- Where do I notice fracture or disconnection—where movement in one sphere strains or drains another?

- How might tending one area—restoring rest, reordering relationships, renewing creative work—begin to ripple across the others?

- What kind of framework, what gentle rule, might help me hold these spheres together as one integrated life before God?

MAY YOUR DAYS BE GATHERED INTO HOLY RHYTHM,

ABIDING IN THE VINE, WHO SUSTAINS ALL THINGS.

PART III

THE EMBODIMENT: LIVING IT OUT

9

WHOLENESS IN THE PRESENCE OF OTHERS

Carry each other's burdens, and in this way you will fulfill the law of Christ.

GALATIANS 6:2

SHE WAS EIGHTY-TWO when she first came to see me—frail, pale, skin like thin paper, hands resting in her lap, as if to steady something deep inside

For years her body had quietly slipped away. Chronic anemia, the chart read. But the chart didn't capture it all: the cascade of hospitalizations, the string of specialists, the endless tests that mapped her body in detail but never told us why. EGD, colonoscopy, tagged red blood cell scans—no one could find the source of the bleed.

Every week now, without fail, she sat across from me, her husband always beside her. We checked labs. Scheduled the next admission. Arranged for another transfusion. The rhythm was weary, familiar, unspoken.

Until one day they came in and the rhythm broke.

She and her husband sat quietly, hands clasped, and told me they were done.

No more transfusions.

No more hospitals.

No more trying to outrun what was coming.

Yet they kept coming—every week, just as before. Not for treatment. Not for interventions. For something else.

We sat. We talked. We prayed.

I checked her labs, the numbers slipping lower—hemoglobin seven, six, five—and still, she came.

Not to be saved.

To be seen.

And then, one week she didn't come.

Her husband called. His voice was steady, kind.

He didn't thank me for the care plan or the medical guidance.

He thanked me for being there.

For showing up when there was nothing left to fix.

For sitting in the quiet with them at the end.

As a physician comprehensively trained to diagnose and find solutions, he presented me with a profound and healing word.

Presence, he reminded me, is sometimes the final and most faithful treatment we can offer.

FORMED FOR COMMUNION

Scripture reminds us—gently but profoundly—that God is not a solitary force who waited to exhale creation into existence. He has always existed in relationship: Father, Son, and Spirit—fully known, fully loving, fully one. A divine communion. A dance of perfect, incorruptible love.

John opens his gospel with this mystery: "In the beginning was the Word, and the Word was with God, and the Word was God. He was with God in the beginning" (John 1:1–2).

The Word—the Son—has always known His Father.

And the Father has always known His Son.

At Jesus's baptism, the Trinity appears again: the Father's voice blessing the Son, the Spirit descending like a dove, the Son standing in the water. Before He teaches, heals, or commissions, the first word spoken over Jesus is love. Not earned. Not achieved. Given, from eternity.

And as Jesus sends out His disciples, He names the communion from which they are sent: "Go, therefore ... in the name of the Father and of the Son and of the Holy Spirit" (Matthew 28:19 ESV).

This is the God who made us—the Breath-Giver, the One who formed dust and filled it with life. When He breathed into us, He gave not just animation but His likeness, His creative joy, His call to steward and shape, and His nature: communal, relational, never alone.

We bear the image of the triune God. We are not just wired for relationship; we are formed for it.

We are incurably relational.

THE WOUND OF DISCONNECTION

But from the moment of the fall, our relationships have been marked by fracture: separation from the Breath-Giver, disintegration within, and disruption with one another.

In Genesis 3, after Adam and Eve eat the fruit, everything changes. They hide from God. They cover themselves. When God calls, Adam's first words are no longer a declaration of union but a distancing: "The woman you put here with me—she gave me some fruit, and I ate it" (Genesis 3:12).

The one he once called "bone of my bone, flesh of my flesh" is now "the woman." The unity they once shared is strained. The tone shifts. Nearness is lost.

This was never how it was meant to be. The triune God knew nothing of hiding, blame, or division. These belong to the fall. Though we were made for communion, we now carry the wound of disconnection.

As relational image-bearers, we carry this ache every day.

We feel it in ways we rarely name: withdrawal, defensiveness, comparison dressed as ambition, performative connection that replaces authentic, vulnerable fellowship. We hunger for belonging but fear what it might cost. We crave intimacy while shielding ourselves from exposure. We live as if we must earn our place in the circle—forgetting we were formed for it from the beginning.

We long to be seen as we truly are—and still be loved. To be chosen without performance. To be safe without pretending.

But we have been trained in mistrust. The serpent's whisper still lingers: *Did God really say ...* And so we protect rather than connect. We withhold. We posture. We stay near but not vulnerable.

Like Adam and Eve hiding in the garden, our fear of exposure often feels stronger than our desire for communion.

This is the paradox of the disintegrated soul: We long for deep connection yet often fear the very intimacy we were created for.

These patterns of protection aren't always conscious. They're woven deep—shaped in the early places of our story: through emotional cues, family systems, and the relationships that taught us what connection costs.

What modern psychology calls *attachment theory* gives language to this shaping.[1] It affirms that the way we first learned to bond and belong shapes how we relate for a lifetime.

Some of us grew up learning that closeness meant comfort, others that it brought danger or disappointment. So we adapted: avoiding, clinging, performing. Not because we're broken but because we were trying to stay safe.

---

1   John Bowlby, *Attachment*, vol. 1 of the Attachment and Loss series (Basic Books, 1969).

THE PHYSICAL COST OF DISCONNECTION

The biblical narrative here is not just poetic—it is physiologically prescient.

"It is not good for man to be alone" wasn't just observation. It was diagnosis. Design.

When we are relationally fractured, the nervous system shifts into chronic alert.

I've seen this play out in patients whose bodies carry the weight of disconnection as much as their minds do: sleep becomes restless, appetite shifts, energy wanes.

Research affirms these realities. The brain's threat centers remain active, cortisol and adrenaline stay elevated, and vagal tone decreases—interrupting our ability to calm, connect, and regulate.[2] Inflammation rises, even at the level of gene expression, as loneliness disrupts immune pathways and fuels chronic disease.[3]

One study, cited by US Surgeon General Vivek Murthy, equated chronic social isolation to smoking fifteen cigarettes a day.[4]

The body lives the ache of the disintegrated nephesh. Even when we refuse to name it, the body bears the cost, and we are living in what some have called the loneliest generation in human history.

In 2023 the CDC reported that more than half of American adults feel emotionally disconnected.[5]

---

2   Stephen W. Porges, *The Polyvagal Theory: Neurophysiological Foundations of Emotions, Attachment, Communication, and Self-Regulation* (W. W. Norton & Company, 2011).

3   Homa Pourriyahi, Niloufar Yazdanpanah, et al., "Loneliness: An Immunometabolic Syndrome," *International Journal of Environmental Research and Public Health* 18, no. 22 (2021): 12162, https://doi.org/10.3390/ijerph182212162.

4   Julianne Holt-Lunstad, Timothy B. Smith, et al., "Loneliness and Social Isolation as Risk Factors for Mortality: A Meta-Analytic Review," *Perspectives on Psychological Science* 10, no. 2 (2015): 227–37, https://pubmed.ncbi.nlm.nih.gov/25910392.

5   Centers for Disease Control and Prevention (CDC), "Health Effects of Social Isolation …" (2024).

Murthy named loneliness as both a cultural concern and a public health crisis—linked to heart disease, dementia, anxiety, depression, and premature death.[6]

This is more than a social problem.

It is the slow unraveling of living souls, itself bearing witness to God's design for integrated wholeness.

And still, despite all we know, the ache remains. Disconnection keeps us guarded. Mistrust keeps us distant. Shame keeps us hidden.

But this isn't the end of the story.

In a world so marked by relational fracture, it's easy to imagine that community is the cure. That it will fix us. That if we can just find the right people, the right group, the right circle, then we will finally feel whole. But community itself is not the source of healing. It is the place where healing unfolds.

Paul reminds us of this in Galatians 6:2: "Carry each other's burdens, and in this way you will fulfill the law of Christ." Yet here lies the tension: We are called to bear with one another, but we so often demand that community carry what it cannot bear—our identity, our validation, our wholeness. And when those expectations fail, the very place meant for healing can become a source of fracture.

Dietrich Bonhoeffer, writing from the shadows of Nazi Germany, understood this. In his brief but piercing book *Life Together*, he wrote about real community—one formed not by chemistry or comfort but by the cross. His words reframe what it means to dwell together as image-bearers and why the healing of the soul cannot be separated from life together with others.

But before authentic community can form, our illusions about it must collapse. "God hates visionary dreaming," Bonhoeffer writes.[7]

Not because vision is inherently bad but because our dreams of

---

6   Vivek H. Murthy, *Our Epidemic of Loneliness and Isolation* (2023).

7   Dietrich Bonhoeffer, *Life Together*, trans. John W. Doberstein (Harper & Row, 1954), 27.

community so often become idols. When we idealize community—when we expect it to meet our needs, mirror our values, or affirm our identity—we set ourselves up for disappointment and for disintegration. We place expectations on others that they were never meant to carry. And when they—or our idealized vision for what community should be—fail, we withdraw.

But Bonhoeffer doesn't see this collapse as failure. He sees it as grace. "He who loves his dream of a community more than the Christian community itself becomes a destroyer of the latter.... The sooner this shock of disillusionment comes to an individual and to a community, the better for both."[8]

Bonhoeffer refers to this disillusionment as the death of the "wish dream"[9]—the idealized vision of Christian community that must be surrendered in order for true fellowship to emerge.

This is not cynicism. It is invitation—the moment when we stop trying to *manufacture* community and begin to *receive* it.

Real belonging does not begin with chemistry or shared opinions. It begins with the cross. With surrender. With shared weakness, not strength.

The death of the wish dream is the beginning of actual presence.

RECLAIMING FELLOWSHIP AS WHOLE SOULS
The death of the wish dream doesn't lead to despair. It leads to grace. When we finally see the failures, the disappointments, the jagged edges of others—or more importantly, they see ours—and resist the urge to run, something holy happens.

---

8   Bonhoeffer, *Life Together*, 27–28.

9   Bonhoeffer, *Life Together*, 26–27.

Bonhoeffer writes, "Just as surely as God desires to lead us to a knowledge of genuine Christian fellowship, so surely must we be overwhelmed by a great disillusionment with others, with Christians in general, and, if we are fortunate, with ourselves."[10]

In that moment—when we see the weakness of another—we're invited into a quiet confession: *me too*. Not in shame but in solidarity. We don't gather as polished souls—we gather as dependent ones, held together by grace rather than perfection.

This is where nephesh takes root in community. We do not relate as minds or beliefs alone. We meet as embodied, breathing, becoming souls—fractured and still being restored. The healing of the soul doesn't happen in sanitized circles. It happens when we look across the table, see someone else's mess ... and stay.

I remember writing to a small group of near strangers early in what would become a decade of walking together. I had just read Bonhoeffer for the first time, and his words on disillusionment struck something deep. I wrote to them with trembling honesty: that I didn't want a perfect group. I didn't expect magic. I just wanted to be part of something real, something that could hold grace when our edges began to show.

And now ten years later, I can say this: Bonhoeffer was right. The dream died. And what remained was better—a fellowship not built on ease but on endurance. On staying. On seeing. On honoring and receiving one another as whole souls in progress.

That is where presence becomes transformative. That is where community becomes communion.

When we live whole before God, we begin to live whole with one another. Living nephesh isn't just about integration within—it's about integration between. We do not meet as souls linked by belief or bodies gathered by proximity or convenience. We meet as image-bearers whose very presence becomes part of God's healing work. In a world

---

10 Bonhoeffer, *Life Together*, 26–27.

of intangible connection and curated spirituality—faith reduced to polished posts or sound bites—the church becomes a radical witness simply by showing up, with hands that serve, arms that hold, voices that pray, meals that feed. Wholeness within makes space for wholeness among. The soul, when restored, makes room for others to rest too.

Within Christian community, we meet as nephesh—whole persons, called to love with more than ideas. The soul that has been restored into harmony with itself extends that same harmony outward—with attentiveness, not perfect words or polished theology.

This kind of nearness is not flashy. It's not about spiritual output or charismatic warmth. It's often quiet, even unseen. But in the life of the living soul, it is sacred work.

We see this in one of Scripture's most tender portraits of care: Elijah under the broom tree.

After a miraculous victory at Mount Carmel, Elijah flees into the wilderness—soul exhausted, body depleted, asking God to take his life. He is not met with rebuke. He is not handed a strategy. He is given rest ... and a meal.

"Get up and eat," the angel says, "for the journey is too much for you" (1 Kings 19:7).

What Elijah received wasn't correction—it was care. The angel meets the prophet's disintegrated nephesh—the collapse of spirit, body, and hope—with gentleness. With food. With stillness. With presence.

This is the shape of healing in Christian community. A quiet willingness to show up, to sit beneath the broom tree, to bring bread. Not advice. Not pressure to rally. To be there when there's nothing left to say.

I've seen it too—not with angels but with a husband who kept showing up beside his wife, even when medicine had nothing more to offer. They no longer came for treatment. They came for presence. And when the visits stopped, he called to say thank you—not for what I did but for simply being there.

This is how wholeness is carried between us—not in performance but in presence. When we show up not as fixers but as fellow image-bearers. When we see not problems to solve but people to hold. When we practice grace in the ordinary rhythms of shared life.

Presence is where healing begins. But presence alone isn't the whole path.

For wholeness to take root, we must risk not only being *with* one another but being *known* by one another.

This is where community deepens. Where trust begins to stretch beyond surface rhythms. Where the soul, still learning how to live whole, dares to step out from hiding.

THE FELLOWSHIP OF CONFESSION

There is a kind of proximity that goes deeper than companionship. One that does not flinch when another's soul is laid bare. The kind that hears the tremble in a voice, sees the flicker of shame, and stays.

Bonhoeffer writes, "He who is alone with his sin is utterly alone."[11]

Confession, he says, is the end of that aloneness. It is the moment when the disintegrated soul dares to become visible again—not before God alone but before another.

This kind of vulnerability is not natural. It is not easy. But it is necessary.

Because **true community is not built on shared strength but on mutual mercy.** It is not held together by agreement or affinity but by grace. And that grace flows most freely when we stop hiding.

In a culture of performance, this feels like death. But it is, in fact, the resurrection life. To confess. To intercede. To be known in our need—this is the soil of soul-deep belonging.

"In confession," Bonhoeffer writes, "the breakthrough to community takes place."[12]

---

11 Bonhoeffer, *Life Together*, 110.

12 Bonhoeffer, *Life Together*, 112.

This is where living nephesh comes full circle—not as a self-contained soul but as a soul restored in the presence of others. We were never meant to live whole in isolation. We are healed not just by God's presence but by His presence through the lives of others.

Because Christ is not only within us.

He is between us.

This is the beauty of the soul restored in community—sustained by grace shared between lives.

And yet for many of us, this is where the ache sharpens. We long for this kind of fellowship. But something within us hesitates. The risk feels too great.

WHEN PRESENCE FEELS IMPOSSIBLE

We do not come to community unscarred. Many of us carry wounds from past churches, strained friendships, silence. We feel the tension—the ache to belong pressed against the instinct to protect. Living nephesh doesn't mean living unafraid. It means noticing the fear and still choosing to stay.

It might mean one risk: inviting someone in, telling the truth, showing up again, asking for prayer. And when you do, it may not be perfect. But it may be real.

And real is where healing begins.

PRACTICING PRESENCE TOGETHER

Wholeness in community doesn't begin with grand gestures. It begins with presence—small, steady, intentional. These practices are not formulas. They are invitations. Ways of gently reorienting our lives toward connection, humility, and grace.

1. SHARE A TABLE

Commit to one regular meal—weekly, biweekly, or monthly—with others.

No agenda. No curriculum. Just togetherness.

Food. Conversation. Laughter. Room for silence.

Let nourishment and belonging grow side by side.

2. CHOOSE ONE ACT OF VULNERABILITY

Name a place of struggle in a safe space.

Ask for prayer. Offer confession. Say aloud, "I've been carrying this."

Let yourself be known, even—perhaps especially—if imperfectly.

3. OFFER AN ACT OF CARE

Show up in a tangible way—bring a meal, write a handwritten note, go for a walk with someone who's weary.

Do it not to fix but to be *with*. Let your body become a vessel of compassion.

4. PRACTICE MUTUAL INTERCESSION

Choose two to three people to pray for consistently—not as an obligation but as a quiet rhythm.

Hold their names before God. Trust that He is weaving your prayers into their wholeness.

5. NOTICE AND STAY

The next time you see sorrow in someone's eyes or silence that feels heavy, pause.

Don't rush in with answers. Don't look away.

Stay present. Breathe. Listen. Sometimes the deepest ministry is staying in the room.

These rhythms don't require a guidebook. Sometimes they're as simple as a pot of meatballs and an open invitation.

Years ago my family started a tradition on Friday nights. We'd open our home to three families—no structure, no agenda, just dinner. Some weeks the table held young parents and retirees. Others, toddlers and high school classmates we barely knew. The conversations were unexpected, sometimes messy, often holy. We called it Friday Night Meatballs, based upon a beautiful article written by Sarah Gray for *Serious Eats*.[13] And in those meals—passed plates and shared stories—the veil between heaven and earth thinned.

Another time, a different table, a now annual tradition: Our small-group men planning a candlelit dinner for our wives. Flowers. Wine pairings. Handwritten notes. We call it Ladies' Night, but it is more than a gesture. It is a declaration: You are seen. You are cherished. You are worth a feast.

And then there's the fire. Once a year we camp out and slow roast a whole hog on my family's land. No rush. No production. Just stories told under stars, living souls nourished by fellowship, smoke, and oak. Friends, neighbors, kids, strangers—over a hundred last year. What

---

13 Sarah Grey, "Friday Night Meatballs: How to Change Your Life With Pasta," *Serious Eats*, August 18, 2014, https://www.seriouseats.com/simpler-entertaining-friday-night-dinners-end-loneliness-how-to-build-community-after-having-kids.

begins as food becomes something else: presence turned tangible. Generations gathered around a sacred flame. A slow-burning kind of communion.

These are not programs. They are practices. They're how we live as whole souls—before God and with one another.

We're not made to heal alone. Wholeness was never meant to be a solitary pursuit—it unfolds in the company of others. To live nephesh is to live *with* and *for* others: as bodies we serve, as stories we carry, as souls we choose to stay beside.

Wholeness grows through life shared—honesty risked, meals offered, sorrows carried together. These are not accessories to the spiritual life.

They *are* the spiritual life.

This is how we begin to live whole, not just within ourselves but among one another.

Pause here.

Breathe in: *Father, Son, Spirit,*

Breathe out: *Teach me to be present.*

Presence does not demand perfection.

It asks for attention.

It begins with staying—at the table, by the bedside, in the silence.

Every time you remain, every time you choose to see and be seen, you join the slow work of God's restoring presence.

REFLECTION: WHOLENESS IN THE PRESENCE OF OTHERS

Find a quiet moment. Breathe deeply. Let your whole self come to rest. Let these questions move gently through you as invitations.

- Where have I experienced the ache of disconnection?

- What wounds still shape how I show up with others?

- Who are the people who have stayed with me, not to fix but to be present?

- What did their presence offer that words could not?

- In what ways have I been hiding—behind performance, silence, or self-protection?

- What small risk of vulnerability might look like a step toward wholeness?

- What rhythms might I begin to practice—around a table, at a bedside, in a shared silence—to embody grace in relationship?

- Where might I need to lay down the "wish dream" of perfect community in order to receive the imperfect gift of real communion?

MAY YOUR SOUL BE FREED FOR JOYFUL COMMUNION, THAT IN BEING HEALED YOU MAY BECOME A SOURCE OF HEALING FOR OTHERS.

10

FAMILIES AS LIVING SOULS

These commandments that I give you today are to be on your hearts. Impress them on your children. Talk about them when you sit at home and when you walk along the road, when you lie down and when you get up.

DEUTERONOMY 6:6-7

SHE WAS STILL A TEENAGER when I met her, but she didn't sit like one. While her mother spoke, her eyes stayed fixed on me—scanning for signs, decoding tone, silently asking questions she hadn't voiced yet. Her posture was taut with the quiet anxiety of someone who'd learned that bad news often came without warning. You could see it in the way she leaned forward just slightly, bracing herself—not for her own diagnosis but for her mother's.

Her own medical chart read like someone three decades older: surgery scars, chronic diagnoses, missed childhood milestones buried beneath a long list of ICD codes. But it was the woman sitting next to her—the one she called "Mama," though their relationship was complex—that explained why she never quite moved like a child.

Her adoptive mother was chronically ill and often volatile. The weight of the household fell squarely on her daughter's shoulders—the chores and cooking and the logistics of survival. They lived with instability—unreliable transportation, a home that barely held out the elements, and little in the way of material support. Still, my patient managed to show up—on time, prepared, composed. The teenager kept her mother's medications organized, her appointments scheduled, her care coordinated.

She asked the questions. She filled out the forms. She learned, somehow, to carry what no child should have to hold.

And then one day it was the mother who arrived alone. She didn't come for care—she came to tell me. Tears spilled freely as she beamed. "She got in. Full scholarship. The university sent her a letter. My baby's going to college. She's gonna be a doctor like you."

Not because it was a tidy success story. But because somehow, in the middle of a system that never offered her wholeness, she became a living soul anyway.

FAMILY AS THE FIRST FORMATION

Before we even know our own name, we are known in a home.

In the hush of early days, our nephesh is molded by tone and touch, warmth and nearness. Or by the ache left when they are missing. Every child is shaped—sometimes by what is given, sometimes by what is withheld.

Here in this first soil, we learn what it means to be a self in relationship with others. What it means to belong. What it means to be safe. What it means to be loved.

We do not choose the place we're born into. It chooses us. The family—however it's made—becomes the first mirror in which we see ourselves. And through that mirror we form answers to questions we don't yet know we're asking: Am I wanted? Am I heard? Is there room for me here?

God, in His wisdom, chose to place human beings not in isolation but in households. Even before Israel was a nation, it was a family—Abraham, Isaac, Jacob. Even before the church became an institution, it was a gathered household of believers breaking bread and sharing burdens. From Genesis onward, God's covenantal work has moved through families: flawed, ordinary, complicated families.

Deuteronomy 6 grounds us in this reality. The Shema—the great prayer of Israel—calls the people to love God with all their nephesh, but also to live that love out loud within the home: "Impress these words on your children. Talk about them when you sit at home and when you walk along the road, when you lie down and when you get up" (Deuteronomy 6:7).

Formation was never meant to happen in the abstract. It was meant to happen in rhythm: in meals, in movement, in rest. God's vision for shaping a whole people was always rooted in in-the-flesh relationships—families less as perfect structures and more as living spaces where the soul can grow.

Of course, we know it doesn't always happen that way.

Just as the fall led to the disintegration of our communion with the Father, so too did it unravel the harmony within ourselves—and within the family. The household, meant to be a place of nurture and belonging, often becomes a space of distortion, silence, or pain.

Our family systems carry the wound.

And yet ... even in that brokenness, God remains present. His Spirit still hovers over the chaos. His breath still moves in and through the stories we carry.

This chapter names that tension—the space between what was intended and what has been lived.

It does not rush to resolve it. But it does bear witness to the possibility of healing.

Not because our families become perfect but because one living nephesh, restored by grace, can begin to make all things new.

WHEN THE SOUL LEARNS TO HIDE

When the garden fractured, so did the home.

The first family after Eden did not flourish in communion—they fractured in silence, rivalry, and grief. Cain and Abel never learned to speak their hearts without violence. And their parents—still reeling from exile—could not teach what they had lost.

That pattern has echoed ever since.

Even today many of us were formed in family systems that were tender, well meaning, yet deeply fractured. The wounds may not have been obvious. They often lived in tone, in absence, in subtle patterns of protection and avoidance. But they shaped us all the same.

And because the soul longs for connection—even in unsafe places—it adapts. It finds ways to stay attached. To be useful. To disappear. These roles are not failures of character. They are survival strategies. The way the nephesh learns to endure what it cannot control.

Psychologists and family systems researchers have long observed that children in fractured or chaotic systems often assume roles to maintain connection—sometimes called the "placater," the "hero," the "lost child." In my own practice, I've seen these same dynamics lived out in ways I'd describe as the "fixer," the "peacekeeper," the "achiever," the "invisible one," and the "caretaker."[1]

Here are just a few of the forms that survival can take:

- THE FIXER. They step in early, absorb tension, anticipate need. They learn to solve problems before they're asked. Their strength is praised but often driven by fear that things will fall apart if they stop holding it all together.

---

1   Similar dynamics are explored in family systems theory (e.g., Virginia Satir, *Conjoint Family Therapy*; Murray Bowen, *Family Therapy in Clinical Practice*; Claudia Black, *It Will Never Happen to Me*) and in Enneagram literature (e.g., Don Richard Riso and Russ Hudson, *The Wisdom of the Enneagram*). My descriptions here synthesize these traditions with observations from practice.

- THE PEACEKEEPER. They manage conflict by dissolving into the background. They keep the room calm at the cost of their own voice. Their presence soothes others but rarely comforts themselves.

- THE ACHIEVER. They earn love through excellence. Their value is tied to performance—grades, behavior, leadership. They glow in public and crumble in private.

- THE INVISIBLE ONE. They lower their needs, minimize their impact, stay out of the way. They become easy children, quiet partners, agreeable adults. And often deeply lonely.

- THE CARETAKER. Especially common among those raised by chronically ill or emotionally unstable parents. They become the adult too soon. They carry what was never theirs and often forget how to be nurtured in return.

None of these roles are inherently wrong. In fact, many carry gifts: empathy, strength, sensitivity, leadership. But when they are *required*—when the system depends on them for stability—they become burdens. Not identities.

These patterns are not randomly assigned. They form in response to the emotional climate of a family. And while therapy offers many helpful models for understanding them, the heart of it is deeply spiritual: The soul that was meant to rest in love learns instead to perform, manage, or disappear.

And yet these roles can be unlearned. Not through blame. Not through backlash. But through the Spirit's gentle work of reformation: naming, releasing, healing.

Returning the soul to something it was always meant to know:

It is safe to be seen. It is not your job to keep the room calm.

You were made to be loved, not managed.

These patterns aren't the invention of modern psychology—they're part of the human condition.

Long before diagnostic labels, they were already shaping families and souls: an ancient inheritance. We see them play out not only in therapy sessions or journal pages but in Scripture itself.

The family of David—beloved king, psalmist, covenant bearer, a man after God's own heart—was a household shaped not only by favor but by fracture.

His story with Bathsheba, though forgiven by God, introduced a tear in the fabric of his nephesh that would echo through his children's lives. The prophet Nathan's words were not a divine punishment but a piercing truth: "The sword shall never depart from your house" (2 Samuel 12:10). The fracture didn't signal God's absence; it exposed that David, in a moment of lust and violence, had abandoned his integrity. And that fracture could not be contained.

Tamar, David's daughter, was raped by her half brother Amnon. And David was angry—but silent. He did not act. Did not comfort her. Did not confront her abuser. And so Tamar was left desolate.

Absalom, Tamar's full brother, carried the rage his father could not express. When justice was denied, he took it into his own hands—murdering Amnon and fleeing into exile. Years passed. David longed for his son yet still refused to see him. And when Absalom was finally brought home, Scripture says that David allowed him to return to the city, but "he must not see my face" (2 Samuel 14:24).

The pain of that sentence reverberates:

A father who could face a giant but not his own son.

A man after God's own heart—whose own heart was absent at home.

Eventually the silence turned to rebellion. Absalom rose against David—not out of entitlement but perhaps out of longing. Longing for justice. For recognition. For his father's presence.

What unfolded was not divine retribution—it was inherited fracture.

Unspoken grief. Unaddressed harm. Unhealed nephesh.

David's failure was not just his initial sin. It was the pattern that followed: His inability to name what had happened. His refusal to confront pain. His silence when his family needed his voice.

These are the same wounds that echo through households today.

When parents carry shame they never speak aloud, their children learn to carry it too.

When trauma is covered instead of confessed, it doesn't disappear—it festers.

And when those in positions of care or power look away, the nephesh of a family slowly unravels.

Trauma doesn't stay contained within a moment. It lingers—in the body, in behavior, in memory. And when left unacknowledged, it doesn't just affect one person—it ripples outward.

Modern research has given us language for what Scripture has long described: That suffering can be transmitted. That wounds can be inherited. That what was left unhealed in one generation often becomes the burden of the next.

The Adverse Childhood Experiences (ACE) study revealed this with startling clarity. Children raised in environments shaped by abuse, addiction, emotional neglect, or chronic instability are at significantly higher risk of nearly every negative outcome—depression, anxiety, autoimmune disease, substance use, relational dysfunction, and even early death.[2] The nephesh, when wounded early and often, adapts in ways that may protect in the short term but fragment over time.

More recently, the field of epigenetics has shown that trauma can actually alter gene expression. The effects of fear, deprivation, and violence are not just emotional—they are biological. Stress-response systems can become overactivated, cortisol regulation disrupted,

---

2   Vincent J. Felitti et al., "Relationship of Childhood Abuse and Household Dysfunction to Many of the Leading Causes of Death in Adults: The Adverse Childhood Experiences (ACE) Study," *American Journal of Preventive Medicine* 14, no. 4 (1998): 245–58, https://doi.org/10.1016/S0749-3797(98)00017-8.

immune function impaired.[3] And these changes can be passed to future generations.

The soul remembers what the mind cannot name.

But trauma doesn't only alter emotion or behavior—it reshapes the body's baseline.

Neuroscience tells us that our nervous systems are formed in the presence of others. A child's capacity to regulate fear, joy, sadness, and stress is not developed in isolation—it is co-regulated through the rhythms of those who raise them.[4]

In this way the household becomes not only a school of belief but a training ground for the nervous system. The tone of a parent's voice, the availability of comfort, the presence or absence of rupture and repair—all these things teach the body what "safe" feels like.

Or how to survive in its absence.

Over time, these cues shape not just the emotional life of the child but the physiological pattern of the nephesh itself. A home marked by unpredictability, volatility, or emotional absence forms a body that stays braced—hypervigilant or numb. A home marked by responsive presence creates a body that knows how to return to rest.

In this sense, trauma is not just what happened. It is what the body had to do to survive what happened.[5]

And this, too, can be passed down.

But Scripture already pointed to this reality, with ancient and

---

3   Rachel Yehuda and Amy Lehmer, "Intergenerational Transmission of Trauma Effects: Putative Role of Epigenetic Mechanisms," *World Psychiatry* 17, no. 3 (2018): 243-57, https://doi.org/10.1002/wps.20568.

4   Bruce D. Perry and Maia Szalavitz, *The Boy Who Was Raised as a Dog: And Other Stories from a Child Psychiatrist's Notebook*, 3rd ed. (Basic Books, 2021), 15–32.

5   Stephen W. Porges, "The Polyvagal Theory: New Insights into Adaptive Reactions of the Autonomic Nervous System," *Cleveland Clinic Journal of Medicine* 76, no. S2 (2009): S86–S90, https://doi.org/10.3949/ccjm.76.s2.17.

profound sharpness. "The parents have eaten sour grapes, and the children's teeth are set on edge" (Jeremiah 31:29).

This isn't blame. It is diagnosis. A recognition that fragmentation, if left unhealed, becomes legacy.

But God's Word doesn't end with that proverb. In the very next breath, the Lord declares that it will not always be so: "Everyone will die for their own sin; whoever eats sour grapes—their own teeth will be set on edge" (Jeremiah 31:30).

The implication is this: The pattern can be broken.

The soul does not have to carry what it did not cause.

What was passed down can be laid down—less by effort, more by healing, presence, honest naming, and grace.

Here's the truth Scripture offers us—not just in the tragedy of David's household but in its redemption: Jesus steps into that very lineage to become the king who restores. He does what David could not:

- He sees the woman who has been bleeding for twelve years—and calls her "daughter."

- He tells stories of a father who runs toward his wayward child, not away.

- He does not avert his face from suffering. He steps into it. He meets it with presence.

- And with His breath—his *ruach*—he makes the broken whole again.

PRACTICING WHOLENESS IN THE FAMILY: SACRED BONDS

Wholeness in the home is not about perfection—it is about presence.

And presence, when sustained with grace and awareness, becomes a healing act.

We are each part of a relational web—some threads tangled, some taut, some tender. This section invites reflection on what it looks like to live nephesh within those relationships not by fixing them but by expressing wholeness within them.

SPOUSE TO SPOUSE

The marriage bond—when lived with mutuality—becomes a space of restoration, not reactivity.

- Practice vulnerability, transparency, and honesty, not just task sharing.

- Invite shared rhythms of prayer or reflection, even if brief.

- Maintain boundaries that protect rest and personhood, not just productivity.

- Choose presence over problem-solving.

A whole marriage isn't a perfect one—it's one in which both souls have room to breathe.

PARENT TO CHILD

Parenting in a nephesh-centered home doesn't aim for control—it aims for *consistency*.

- Prioritize rhythm over perfection: morning snuggles, evening blessing, shared meals.

- Offer blessing aloud: not praise for performance but words of identity.

- Re-parent where needed—offering your child what you were never given.

- Let grace interrupt cycles of shame.

The gift of nephesh parenting is not that your child has a flawless home but that they *never* have to wonder whether they are loved.

CHILD TO PARENT

Many adults carry invisible weight in their relationship with a parent—especially when that parent remains emotionally unhealed, distant, or unaware of the harm they've caused. The pressure to remain silent, agreeable, or endlessly accommodating can linger long after childhood has ended.

Living nephesh in this relationship means recognizing that honor and health are not opposites. You can choose wholeness without choosing hostility.

- Forgiveness may mean releasing the inner demand for an apology that may never come—not because it wasn't needed but because your soul needs to be free.

- Boundaries protect your capacity to stay present without losing yourself. They clarify what you will and will not carry.

- Chosen grace is offering kindness that is real, not performative. It's a gift—an overflow, not a duty—and it must include care for your own nephesh.

- You are allowed to stop playing the role you learned in childhood. Whether that was fixer, caretaker, peacekeeper, high achiever, or invisible one, you no longer have to sacrifice yourself in order to stay connected.

SIBLING TO SIBLING

Sibling relationships are often the longest we carry—stretching from our earliest memories to the end of life. In many homes, roles form not in isolation but in reaction to one another: the responsible one, the rebellious one, the quiet one, the golden child.

Living nephesh in sibling dynamics means honoring the significance of those bonds—through patient tending of the patterns they formed instead of pressing for closeness.

- ACKNOWLEDGE THE ROLES YOU PLAYED. The caretaker, the competitor, the overlooked one. These roles often emerge in reaction to one another and can silently shape our sense of identity for decades.

- NAME ANY GRIEF OR HARM. Sibling wounds are often minimized, but they matter—emotional distance, favoritism, betrayal, estrangement. Healing begins when we stop pretending they didn't leave a mark.

- RELEASE THE COMPARISON. If you learned to measure your worth against a sibling, let the Spirit reframe your story. You were never meant to be defined in contrast to another soul.

- EXTEND FORGIVENESS–OR CREATE PEACE. You may not reconcile fully, but you can choose to stop carrying resentment. You can bless from a distance. You can set down what was never yours to hold.

- MAKE SPACE FOR SOMETHING NEW. As adults, sibling bonds can evolve. With grace and boundaries, new rhythms of connection may begin—not rooted in nostalgia but in presence.

Your sibling relationships may never become what you once hoped. But they can still be touched by healing, softened by grace, or gently released in peace.

This kind of healing may leave the relationship unrepaired, yet it restores the soul.

WITHIN THE LARGER FAMILY SYSTEM

Even when dysfunction remains, one whole person can become a steadying presence.

- Kindness without codependence.

- Invitations without emotional manipulation.

- Rhythm without resentment.

Wholeness doesn't mean everyone is healed. It means someone chose to be whole in the presence of fracture.

Change doesn't come easily, especially in the systems that formed us. Resistance is normal. Naming the barriers can be a first act of freedom.

- Family of origin wounds that still press against the present.

- Over-identification or detachment: swinging between enmeshment and emotional exile.

- Differing levels of spiritual maturity between family members.

- Unspoken rules and inherited survival strategies that whisper, "We don't talk about that" or "Don't make it worse."

- The myth that love equals fixing, which leads to burnout and quiet resentment.

- The fatigue of carrying what others won't acknowledge.

Think of this not as indictment but as gentle naming of why this is difficult. Healing is not resisted because it's wrong but because it's different.

WHAT IT LOOKS LIKE TO BEGIN AGAIN

You do not have to heal your whole family.

But your wholeness creates space for theirs.

Here are some practices—invitations rather than prescriptions—to cultivate living nephesh within the home:

- SHARED SABBATH (even if it's just a meal or a screen-free hour)

- BLESSING AT MEALS—a word of gratitude or a phrase spoken aloud over those present

- RHYTHMS OF PRAYER—morning "God, be with us," or evening "Thank you for today"

- REGULAR CONFESSION AND REPAIR—"I was harsh today. I'm sorry. Will you forgive me?"

- SPEAKING SACRED WORTH ALOUD—naming identity beyond behavior: "You are loved. I see you."

- NAMING GRACE WITHOUT DEMANDING CHANGE—giving freedom rather than pressure

- HOSPITALITY—creating space for others, both literal and emotional

You are not responsible for everyone else's healing.

You are invited to be a living soul in the room.

You can be a presence that carries rest.

And that, over time, changes everything.

And while no one emerges from family untouched, and we are all shaped by the households that formed us—whether through love that anchored us or silence that taught us to disappear—we carry forward memories and patterns. Survival strategies. Ghosts of roles we learned too early. Longings still unmet.

And yet the story doesn't end with what we inherited.

In Christ we are not bound to repeat what was passed down. He steps into the fractured line of David—to redeem the pain, not erase it.

To be the healing presence where absence once ruled.

To give us what our parents couldn't.

To show us how to bless our children differently.

To remind us that wholeness is not a solo project but a shared restoration sustained by grace.

You are not responsible for your entire family's healing. But your wholeness can create space for theirs. Not by controlling the outcome but by becoming a steady presence. By breathing deeply instead of bracing. By choosing truth and tenderness, even when others stay silent. By offering your care, your kindness, your boundaries, your belonging.

This is the way of the living nephesh:

To carry the breath of God into the places we were once afraid to enter.

To become whole—and in doing so, to make healing possible for others.

It begins with one soul.

It begins with yours.

Pause here.

Breathe in: *I am not what I've had to carry.*

Breathe out: *Make me a healing presence, O God.*

Wholeness at home is not perfection.

It is space—space for rest, for truth, for grace.

Each gentle breath, each act of forgiveness, each steady kindness becomes shelter.

You cannot force another's healing, but you can live in a way that makes it possible.

REFLECTION: A GUIDED EXAMEN FOR THE FAMILY SOUL

Find a quiet place. Breathe deeply. Ask the Spirit to guide you. Then slowly walk through these steps:

1. GRATITUDE

   Look back over your life this week or this season.

   Where have you experienced love, connection, or unexpected grace in your family life—past or present?

   Was there a moment of laughter, of warmth, of being seen?

   Give thanks, even if the moment was small.

2. PRESENCE

   Where have you recently felt most grounded in your relationships?

   Where did you feel most reactive, guarded, or disconnected?

   Notice without judgment.

   What did your body do in those moments—tense, withdraw, soften?

3. INHERITANCE

What roles did you learn to play in your family?

Do you notice yourself still playing them today?

Where are you carrying something that wasn't yours to hold?

Were you compared to a sibling growing up? How did that shape you?

Is there a sibling you need to forgive—or grieve?

Name what was passed down, both the gifts and the burdens.

4. CONFESSION AND RELEASE

Where have you withheld presence—from yourself, your children, your spouse, your parents?

Where are you still trying to fix or manage what is not yours to carry?

Offer those places to God.

Release the illusion of control and let grace hold what you cannot.

5. INVITATION

Where is God inviting you to live as a healing presence?

Is there a rhythm, a boundary, a word of blessing, or a letting-go that you're being called to practice?

Listen for a next step—not to fix your family but to remain whole within it.[6]

MAY THE WHOLENESS YOU RECEIVE BECOME WHOLENESS SHARED, BRINGING HEALING WITHIN YOUR FAMILY.

---

6   If you'd like a visual and reflective companion to this practice, appendix D offers the Family Soul Map. It's a simple tool designed to help you name the stories, patterns, roles, and relationships that shaped you—and begin to discern where God might be inviting healing within your family system.

11

BECOMING WHOLE IN SUFFERING

He restores my soul.

PSALM 23:3 ESV

SHE ENTERED MY OFFICE SLOWLY—always slowly.

Forearm crutches braced each step, her gait uneven, her movements deliberate. Her body carried the story of decades: past addiction, bone infections, surgeries that never quite fixed what they'd set out to heal. Her hips were nearly gone. Her spine stiff. Pain clung like a shadow, and so did the medications required to manage it.

And yet ... she shone.

There was a quiet radiance about her. Not denial. Not cheerfulness. But a kind of settled joy that surprised you if you were not paying attention. She didn't pretend she was okay. She didn't hide the limp. She just came—open, grounded, gracious.

She talked about Jesus like He was in the room.

She listened carefully. Laughed easily. Wept when she needed to, sometimes midsentence.

Sometimes she brought a verse written on a scrap of paper. Sometimes a prayer request for someone else in the waiting room.

She was, by every clinical measure, chronically ill.

But when she left, the room felt more whole.

Somehow—despite everything—she had become a living soul.

Not because she had been made pain-free.

But because she had learned how to carry the presence of God in a body that still broke.

SEASONS WHEN THE RHYTHMS BREAK

When the practices you've built no longer hold—when the breath grows shallow, the body aches without explanation, or a diagnosis rewrites your daily life—you may find yourself in the bed or sitting beside it.

In these seasons, wholeness can feel impossibly distant, like a fading memory—or worse, like a concept that was never meant for you.

Maybe it's chronic pain that wears down the edges of your soul. Fatigue that no amount of sleep lifts.

Maybe you're living on the other side of a diagnosis—or walking through the quiet grief of watching someone you love disappear into illness, addiction, or decline.

This is not the part of the story we want to stay in.

But some of us don't have a choice.

And here's the truth that so few know how to say aloud: Suffering can disintegrate you. It can pull apart the threads of body and spirit. It can make you question who you are when you no longer move, work, parent, serve, or speak the way you once did.

You are not weak for feeling this. You are human.

Even the strongest soul will strain under the weight of illness, grief, or unresolved pain.

Even the most faithful will wonder whether they are still whole when they can no longer feel God's presence in the same way—or feel anything at all.

But here is where the deep work begins.

Because suffering—though it shatters—can also strip away the roles, identities, and illusions we've layered over our soul.

And beneath what has been broken, something essential remains:

You are still a living soul.

Still made in the image of God.

Still loved.

Still carried by grace.

Wholeness does not mean you will return to how you were.

It means you are being made whole in a way you may not yet understand.

HE RESTORES THE SOUL–EVEN HERE

One of the internal witnesses to the trustworthiness of Scripture is its honesty.

It doesn't gloss over grief. It doesn't flatten the pain. From Genesis to Revelation, the story of God's people is not one of ease—it's one of endurance. Jesus Himself promised that in this world we would have trouble. But He also promised that He would be with us in it.

Scripture is not a book of perfect people who found easy answers.

It's a love story of a faithful God who walks with fragile souls. Sarah. Hagar. Hannah. Job. David. Elijah. Esther. Paul. Even Jesus. The pattern is not avoidance of pain—it is presence *within* it. And again and again, God brings glory from the wounded places.

In Psalm 23 David writes from the valley, from the shadow itself. He speaks as one surrounded by the threat of death. And yet he holds fast to what he knows of the Shepherd: "He restores my soul" (Psalm 23:3 ESV).

In Hebrew: *nephesh.*

And this restoration doesn't come once David escapes the valley—it happens within it.

After the resurrection, Jesus didn't return to His disciples radiant with untouchable perfection. He came back with wounds. He invited Thomas to touch the scars. His glorified body could have been unmarred—but it wasn't.

Why?

Because **the glory of God isn't shown in erasure. It's shown in** *redemption*.

There are countless moments in Scripture where God is glorified not despite the wound but through it:

- Job cries out in bitterness and grief—and still, God is near.

- Elijah collapses in fear and fatigue—and God meets him with food and presence.

- Paul pleads for the thorn to be removed—and God doesn't take it away. He simply says, "My grace is sufficient" (2 Corinthians 12:9).

God does not always heal the body. He never promised He would.

What He does promise is restoration of the nephesh—a return to communion, to belonging, to the breath that once filled dust and made it live—just as He declared through Ezekiel: "I will give you a new heart ... and I will put my Spirit in you" (Ezekiel 36:26–27).

He restores the soul. Not only in triumph but in trial. Not after the wound is healed but while it still aches.

And He offers not just healing—but presence. He sits with us beside the coals of despair. He enters the shadow with us.

And as the psalmist writes, He draws near to the brokenhearted (Psalm 34:18, author's paraphrase).

WHEN THE NEPHESH GROANS

Pain doesn't just affect the body—it alters memory, identity, presence, prayer. Grief doesn't just break your heart—it fogs your attention, flattens your affect, reshapes your rhythms. Fatigue doesn't just slow you down—it can make the sacred feel distant.

It's not that the body suffers while the soul floats free—it's that the nephesh suffers all at once.

Whole-person disintegration.

When illness drags on. When caregiving becomes a daily identity. When mental health spirals or diagnosis reorders life. We don't just lose function—we lose the sense of who we are.

You might forget what delight feels like. You might begin to believe you're just a burden. You might wonder where God went or why you can no longer find your old ways of connecting with Him.

And yet your nephesh remains.

Still alive beneath the ache. Still worthy of restoration. Still capable of connection, even if the form looks different now.

What Jesus promises in suffering is not that you'll get your life back. It's that you'll be met. That your soul can still breathe, though your breath may be shallow. That your identity is not in what you can produce, fix, or perform—but in who holds you.

Even here, you are becoming whole.

WHAT THE LIVING NEPHESH ALREADY KNOWS

Wholeness in suffering is not a theological fantasy. It's a lived reality documented in both Scripture and the human experience.

Modern psychology gives us language for something ancient: Healing does not always mean the removal of pain. Sometimes it means the reintegration of the self in the presence of pain.[1] Research

---

1   John A. Sturgeon, "Psychological Therapies for the Management of Chronic Pain," *Psychology Research and Behavior Management* 7 (2014): 115–24, https://doi.org/10.2147/PRBM.S44762.

in post-traumatic growth (PTG) has shown that people who walk through intense suffering do not always end up diminished. In fact, many develop

- a deeper sense of personal strength;

- greater appreciation for life;

- more intimate relationships;

- a clearer sense of purpose;

- and—in many cases—a more grounded spirituality.[2]

They are not "recovered." They are re-formed—not unscarred but more deeply alive.

The themes described in PTG research—personal strength, renewed appreciation of life, new possibilities, deeper relationships, and spiritual change—often echo keystone words within Scripture and Christian theology, such as *endurance, renewal, reorientation,* and *redemption*.[3] It validates what we see in Job, Paul, and the story of the cross: Suffering doesn't always produce clarity but it can produce character. Meaning. And even wholeness.

As James wrote: "Consider it pure joy, my brothers and sisters, whenever you face trials of many kinds, because you know that the testing of your faith produces perseverance. Let perseverance finish its

---

2   Reema Chande, "Post-Traumatic Growth: Fostering Positive Psychological Change," Remedy, February 24, 2025, https://remedypsychiatry.com/post-traumatic-growth-fostering-positive-psychological-change/.

3   Richard G. Tedeschi and Lawrence G. Calhoun, "Posttraumatic Growth: Conceptual Foundations and Empirical Evidence," *Psychological Inquiry* 15, no. 1 (2004): 1–18.

work so that you may be mature and complete, not lacking anything"
(James 1:2–4).

NARRATIVE IDENTITY AND CHRONIC ILLNESS

Sociologist Arthur Frank has described how illness breaks the continuity of the self—it interrupts the story we thought we were living.[4] But healing does not mean returning to the old plotline. It means learning to tell a new one.

Those who suffer deeply often come to re-author their lives with new language: a shift from "Why is this happening?" to "Who am I now—and how do I live as a whole person in this?"

We were created by an Author who delights in giving new stories— not ones that erase the pain but ones that transfigure it.

And we were built with hearts eager to receive them.

This is not about romanticizing pain. It's about reclaiming agency within it. And that reclamation is a form of nephesh restoration—not because the pain is gone but because the person has been remembered.

SPIRITUALITY, SUFFERING, AND THE LIVING SOUL

Study after study confirms what the faithful have long known: People with spiritual grounding tend to navigate illness and trauma with greater resilience not because they are in denial but because they are anchored.[5] They carry a sense of meaning that can hold their suffering without reducing it.

Dr. Harold Koenig's work on spiritual health has shown that

---

4   Arthur W. Frank, *The Wounded Storyteller: Body, Illness, and Ethics* (University of Chicago Press, 1995).

5   Harold G. Koenig, "Religion, Spirituality, and Health: The Research and Clinical Implications," *ISRN Psychiatry* (2012): 1–33, https://doi.org/10.5402/2012/278730.

practices like prayer, Scripture engagement, and even simple rituals—like lighting a candle or whispering a breath prayer—can reduce anxiety, improve pain tolerance, and deepen relational connection.[6]

In other words: the presence of God matters.

The soul is not abstract. It is lived and breathed. It is embodied.

And when it is tended with grace, it remembers how to be whole.

To live as a living nephesh is not to live without wounds.

It is to live whole—even while unhealed.

Cultural narratives often equate wholeness with recovery. But living nephesh does not mean your symptoms have resolved. It doesn't mean the pain is gone, the relationships mended, or that you feel God clearly every morning.

It means something quieter, deeper:

That you are not fragmented in your response to suffering.

That you are not lost to yourself.

That you are not alone.

When your days revolve around appointments; lab results; long, quiet hospital hallways; or the other side of the bed remaining empty, it's easy to feel your identity collapse into a single word: Patient. Widower. Survivor. Caregiver.

But that is not your truest name.

God whispers to remind you: You were made for more.

You are more than a diagnosis. More than your limitations. Your worth has never been tied to clarity, productivity, or emotional steadiness.

With Jesus, it has never been about what you can do. It has always been about what He has already done. To be a living nephesh in suffering may mean simply this:

to stay present in the pain;

to speak the truth about where it hurts;

to abide in the Vine, even when the valley is long.

---

6 Koenig, "Religion, Spirituality, and Health," 1–33.

Wholeness here means honest presence. It means asking for help without shame. It means letting your soul remember that God is still with you—sometimes through your own breath, sometimes through the hands of others.

It looks like accepting kindness you cannot repay;

letting someone else hold your sorrow for a while;

recognizing that weeping, breathing, or sitting in silence are themselves acts of worship.

God is not absent in these moments. He is folded into them.

Wholeness also looks like slow faithfulness—not dramatic acts of courage but small, sustaining movements:

letting someone else carry the load,

letting Scripture meet you in the ordinary,

letting your breath become your prayer,

letting rest become an act of trust.

These are the quiet rhythms that remind you that you are still here, and you are still His.

And finally, wholeness is held together by grace, not willpower.

You are not responsible for fixing your life.

You are not failing because you are not healed.

You are not too broken to be loved.

You are still a living soul.

You are still worthy.

PRACTICING PRESENCE IN PAIN

Wholeness in suffering is not something you achieve. It's something you return to again and again. A lived rhythm. A slow remembering.

These practices are not prescriptions. They are invitations. You may not have the strength to engage them all. You're not meant to. But perhaps one will meet you in this season—a breath, a word, a flicker of light.

Let them be gentle. Let them be small.

The soul doesn't need performance.

It needs presence.

1. LIGHT A CANDLE

    On the days when prayer feels unreachable, light a candle.

    Let it speak for you. Let it say: *God, I am still here. Meet me in this flame.*

    This small act can carry more meaning than words—especially in moments when you have none.

    Let the warmth remind you:

    You are not forsaken.

    Even in silence, you are seen.

2. PAIR A PSALM WITH YOUR MEDICATION

    As you reach for your pills, reach also for a line of Scripture.

    Not to force healing but to hold on to hope.

    - "The Lord is my Shepherd."

    - "You restore my soul."

    - "My grace is sufficient for you."

    Let your soul and your body receive care together.

    There is no hierarchy between them in the kingdom of God.

3. SIT IN SILENCE—AND CALL IT WORSHIP

You do not need eloquence to be with God.

Sit. Breathe. Let your tears fall if they come. Let your mind wander and return.

This, too, is grace.

You are not failing.

This is still communion.

You are still abiding.

4. LET OTHERS CARRY YOU

There will be days when your strength falters. Let someone else bring the meal, send the text, pray the prayer.

You are not a burden. You are part of a body.

Even Jesus let Simon carry the cross for a while.

5. PRACTICE GENTLE TOUCH

Place your hand over your heart. Or rest it on your forehead.

Breathe slowly, and speak this blessing over your own body: "You are still here. You are still mine. You are not too broken to belong."

Your body is part of your nephesh. Treat it with the kindness you would offer a suffering friend.

No one chooses suffering. But many of us wake up in its presence. And while we may long for healing, living nephesh reminds us:

God's aim is not just symptom relief—it is soul restoration.

He does not wait for us to be unscarred before He draws near.

He meets us in the wound.

You do not need to return to who you were.

You do not need to hide the limp or pretend you're okay.

You are allowed to live as a whole person—here, within the valley.

Wholeness in suffering comes through presence, not effort. God's and your own.

Even in the ache, even in the slowness, even in the silence—

He restores the soul.

You are still a living nephesh.

Still beloved.

Still becoming whole.

NEPHESH LIVING

Pause here.

Breathe in: *You restore my soul.*

Breathe out: *Even here, I am whole.*

REFLECTION: A BLESSING FOR THE BODY THAT STILL HURTS

Find a quiet place. Let your hands rest on your lap or over your heart.

Breathe slowly. You do not need to be fixed to be whole.

These words are for you.

May you know that your pain is not a disqualification but a doorway to presence.

May you feel God not only in your strength but in your sorrow.

Not only in your clarity but in your questions.

To your feet, which carry pain and weariness—you are not weak. You are still traveling.

May you be blessed with steadiness, even if the ground is uneven.

May you be honored for the miles you've walked.

To your hands, which shake or swell or grow tired—you are not failing.

May you be blessed for what you still hold, and for what you've had to release.

To your breath, which sometimes falters—you are still the sign of life.

May you be blessed with gentleness, not force.

May you inhale mercy and exhale release.

To your nervous system, stretched and frayed—you have worked so hard to offer protection.

May you be blessed with moments of safety.

May you relearn what peace feels like.

To your scars, visible or hidden—you are not shameful.

May you be blessed as witnesses to survival.

May you remember that healing is not erasure.

To your whole being—your nephesh—you are still beloved. Still here. Still becoming whole.

May you be blessed not for your strength but for your willingness to stay.

Let your hands rest open for a moment.

There is nothing you need to prove.

MAY YOU REMEMBER THAT THIS BODY IS YOUR HOME.

AND THE BREATH-GIVER IS ALREADY HERE.

12

EMBODIED STEWARDSHIP

*Therefore, I urge you, brothers and sisters, in view of God's mercy, to offer
your bodies as a living sacrifice, holy and pleasing to God—this is your true
and proper worship.*

ROMANS 12:1

SHE USED TO CALL HERSELF "GOOD" OR "BAD," depending on how many
carbs she'd eaten that day.

Fifty-something, postmenopausal, and endlessly tired—her medical
chart read like a rotating greatest hits of diet culture: South Beach,
Atkins, Weight Watchers, E2M. Each new start brought a burst of
intensity—strict meal plans, color-coded containers, even two-a-day
workouts before and after work. It was discipline but not devotion. It
was punishment cloaked in pursuit.

She lost weight, sometimes dramatically. But always it returned—
along with her elevated blood sugar, her cholesterol, and the quiet ache
of shame she carried behind her well-rehearsed optimism. Somewhere

along the way, food stopped being nourishment. Her body stopped feeling like home.

But lately, something was changing.

The language had shifted—not from "cheat days" to "clean eating" but to something quieter, something more rooted. She'd begun embracing meals that grow from the ground—olive oil, roasted vegetables, legumes, grains. Not for the scale but for the soul. She called it a lifestyle now, not a diet. She no longer weighed every ounce or tracked every macro. She ate slowly, sometimes with music playing. Sometimes with prayer.

Her workouts weren't punishment anymore. She lifted weights, walked outside, breathed more deeply. She still had goals, but they no longer demanded violence against her body. They invited communion with it.

And though the change was slow—slower than any program ever promised—she sensed a steadiness about it. Her labs were improving. Her body was softening toward itself. She was not just managing her health. She was tending her soul.

For the first time in a long time, she was becoming whole again—one bite, one breath, one slow walk at a time.

A THEOLOGY OF EMBODIED WORSHIP

She is not alone. So many of us inherit the belief—whether from church culture, wellness culture, or somewhere in between—that our bodies are obstacles to be overcome. Something to master. Something to tame. Even when our theology affirms that we are "fearfully and wonderfully made" (Psalm 139:14), our day-to-day habits reveal a quieter assumption: The body is a liability.

But this has never been the witness of Scripture.

In the beginning, God formed the human body with His hands. He didn't speak us into being from a distance—He gathered the dust. He shaped it. Then with breath on His lips, He bent low and filled that dust with His Spirit. Only then did the human become nephesh: a living, breathing soul. Not a soul trapped inside a body. Not a spiritual essence waiting to be freed. A unified whole—spirit and body, breath and dust, fully alive in the presence of God.

The apostle Paul echoes this wholeness when he writes, "Offer your bodies as a living sacrifice ... this is your true and proper worship" (Romans 12:1). Worship is not confined to the sanctuary. It takes place in kitchens and walking trails, in grocery aisles and at dinner tables. It lives in the way we nourish, move, and rest. To offer our bodies is not merely to restrain them but to attend to them. To dignify them. To steward them as sacred space.

To live nephesh is to reject two false gospels:

- One that says the body doesn't matter—that it's irrelevant, inferior, or even shameful.

- And one that says the body is everything—that performance, appearance, and optimization define our worth.

Both are distortions. Both fracture us. In contrast, the biblical story calls us not to conquer the body or idolize it but to *inhabit* it—with reverence and presence.

Your body is the very place where your spiritual life is lived—its dwelling, not its accessory.

FOOD FROM THE GARDEN: WHAT WE EAT AS WORSHIP

Food is not just fuel. It is formational. Every bite we take participates in a rhythm of creation, culture, and care—either drawing us closer to the design of the Breath-Giver or further from it.

In the garden of Eden, God surrounded humanity with food that was "pleasing to the eye and good for food" (Genesis 2:9). Not engineered or optimized. Not forbidden or feared. Beautiful, whole, abundant. Food was given as a *gift*, not a test. A source of strength and shared joy—not shame.

We live far from Eden now. Most of us eat not from soil but from packaging—refined, preserved, and distanced from its source. Many of us were raised not to bless our food but to distrust it, to track it, or to moralize it. "Good" food and "bad" food. "Cheat" meals and "clean" days. But this kind of relationship with food fractures us. It fuels cycles of control, guilt, and disembodiment. And it does not lead to wholeness.

But there is another way.

The best clinical evidence continues to affirm what Scripture already whispered: that food close to creation—whole, plant rich, minimally processed—is the kind that heals.[1] Mediterranean and whole-food plant-based diets are linked to lower rates of cardiovascular disease, diabetes, obesity, and inflammation. They reduce anxiety and depression, improve gut-brain health, and stabilize energy and mood.[2] These aren't fad diets. They are wisdom patterns, grounded in biology, not trends.

And when we align our eating with this kind of wisdom, as a grace-filled rhythm, we participate in a kind of repentance. A return. We reject the narrative of scarcity and control and instead embrace food as a form of worship: a daily act of stewardship, of trust, of celebration.

This doesn't mean we all must become vegetarians. But it does mean we might ask this: What kind of food forms the kind of soul I want to become?

Choosing mostly plants is not a rule. It's a practice of remembering the garden. It's a way of tending to the body with the same gentleness God used when He shaped the first one. It's slow and quiet and kind. And it can heal not just your labs but your life.

Let your table be a place of blessing again. Not control. Not calculation. But wholeness.

---

1 Yanping Wang, Bing Liu, et al., "Associations Between Plant-Based Dietary Patterns and Risks of Type 2 Diabetes, Cardiovascular Disease, Cancer, and Mortality: A Systematic Review and Meta-Analysis," *Nutrition Journal* 22, no. 1 (2023): 46, https://doi.org/10.1186/s12937-023-00877-2.

2 Alyona G. Lee et al., "Exploring Plant-Based Diets and Mental Health Outcomes: A Systematic Review," *Cureus* 17, no. 8 (2025): e89846, https://doi.org/10.7759/cureus.89846.

HOW WE EAT: RECLAIMING THE TABLE

Eating is both content and context. *What* we eat shapes the body; *how* we eat shapes the soul.

For many of us, eating has become a solitary, distracted, or anxious act—something squeezed between appointments, consumed in cars, or done while scrolling. Even for the faithful, the table is often just another task to manage. But in Scripture the table is never just about food. It is about fellowship, formation, and the presence of God.

From the garden to the wilderness to the upper room, God has always met His people at meals. Jesus, in particular, seemed to do most of His ministry at the table. He ate with tax collectors and sinners, broke bread with His disciples, multiplied food for the crowds. He didn't just preach the kingdom—He tasted it, blessed it, and shared it.

And this sacred pattern is echoed in some of the healthiest cultures in the world—places like Ikaria, Sardinia, and Okinawa, often called "Blue Zones." In these communities, people don't just eat the right foods; they eat them the right way: slowly, communally, with gratitude. Meals are lingered over, filled with conversation and laughter. Food becomes more than sustenance—it becomes a celebration of connection and a practice of presence. Longevity and vitality in these regions are not simply a product of nutritional content but of a way of life that honors the table as a place of blessing.[3]

To reclaim our wholeness, we must reclaim the table. Not through picture-perfect presentations but through presence. Through slowness. Through intentional gratitude.

When we give thanks before a meal, we are not performing a ritual—we are practicing alignment. Naming that what we are about to eat is not our own doing. That we are sustained by mercy, not macros. This

---

3   Dan Buettner and Suzanne Skemp, "Blue Zones: Lessons from the World's Longest Lived," *American Journal of Lifestyle Medicine* 10, no. 5 (2016): 318–21, https://doi.org/10.1177/1559827616637066.

is where stewardship becomes worship. Intentional practices of eating as wholeness might include these:

- Sitting down for meals, even if they're simple.

- Turning off screens.

- Chewing slowly, breathing between bites.

- Saying grace not as a ritual we perform but as a rhythm that forms us.

- Inviting others to the table, even when it's imperfect.

And when we eat together, something sacred happens. The hurried body slows. The divided soul integrates. The fragmented day gathers into one moment of connection.

You don't need perfect ingredients or a Michelin star–worthy plate. You just need presence. Because when we eat with gratitude, in alignment with God's design and with the people He's given us, the table becomes more than nourishment. It becomes communion.

MOVEMENT AS DEVOTION, NOT DISCIPLINE

For much of modern culture, movement has become synonymous with metrics—steps, reps, calories burned. We've turned exercise into a form of penance, something to earn our food or justify our rest. But movement was never meant to be punishment. It was meant to be presence.

Before the fall, the first humans didn't sit still. They walked with God in the garden. They named, tended, cultivated, carried. Their movement was not about body image—it was about *belonging*. It was life lived in rhythm with creation.

Their movement was not toil; it was delight. Work was not burden but worship.

To live nephesh means reclaiming movement as a form of devotion, not discipline. A return to the joy of being alive. This might look like

- walking slowly after a meal;

- lifting weights with intention, not self-loathing;

- stretching in silence before bed;

- doing chores with mindfulness, as an act of service;

- dancing in the kitchen or kneeling in prayer.

For some, movement is limited by illness, fatigue, or pain. But even the smallest act—stretching the hands, breathing deeply, sitting upright in gratitude—can be movement with meaning. The goal is not intensity. It is *integration*.

We move to show up for our lives, not to shrink ourselves.

To celebrate the body that receives food, not to earn it.

To participate, not to perfect.

Let your body move to remember its worth, not to prove it.

REST AND RHYTHM: TRUSTING WITH OUR TIME

If movement is how we participate in creation, rest is how we return to the Creator.

In a world obsessed with productivity, rest feels unnatural—sometimes even shameful. We resist it, avoid it, numb ourselves instead of entering it. But from the beginning, rest was not an afterthought. It was the culmination of creation. On the seventh day, God rested—not because He was tired but because His work was whole. And He called that day "holy" (Genesis 2:2).

Our bodies were never meant to run without pause. But many of us treat rest as a luxury rather than a necessity. We grind through the week, collapse on weekends, and wonder why we feel disconnected from God, from others, and from ourselves.

Rest is not laziness. It's not indulgence. It's trust.

To rest is to say, *I am not the center of the universe.*

To sleep is to say, *The world will keep turning without me.*

To Sabbath is to say, *God is God, and I am not.*

When we ignore rest, we begin to fracture. Cortisol rises. Sleep cycles break. Our minds race while our bodies revolt. But when we return to rhythm—daily, weekly, seasonally—we begin to heal.

Wholeness requires margin. It requires downtime. And it requires the humility to believe that grace does not depend on our output.

Some practices of whole-person rest might include these:

- Keeping one day each week screen-free and slow.

- Building an evening ritual of stretching, breath prayer, or stillness.

- Honoring the body's signals: hunger, fatigue, pain—not as annoyances but as invitations.

- Taking walks without headphones. Napping without guilt.

You don't have to earn your rest.

You were made for it.

And when we practice it, we return to the pattern of Eden—where time itself was not an enemy but a gift.

NEPHESH LIVING

Pause here.

Breathe in: *This body is yours.*

Breathe out: *This life is worship.*

Your body is not an afterthought.

It is the place where God's Spirit dwells, the vessel through which love becomes touch, presence, and action.

To tend your strength, your limits, your rhythms is not self-focus—it is stewardship.

Every stretch, every meal received with gratitude, every boundary honored in rest is an offering.

To live embodied is to say with your whole nephesh: Here I am, Lord. Use me—dust and breath—for your glory.

REFLECTION: TENDING THE TEMPLE

Wholeness doesn't arrive all at once.

It is formed in the small, repeated choices we make with our bodies—how we eat, how we move, how we rest. These choices are not just health behaviors. They are soul practices.

And when we approach them not with shame or pressure but with presence, they become acts of worship.

You don't need a perfect routine. You need a faithful rhythm.

Use this simple daily reflection to return to your body with grace:

- Did I nourish my body with gratitude and intention today? (What did I eat? How did I feel? Was it a moment of care?)

- Did I move with presence, not pressure? (Did I stretch, walk, lift, carry, breathe? Did it reconnect me to myself?)

- Did I rest with trust? (Did I listen to my fatigue? Did I slow down at all?)

- Did I speak kindly to my body—or silently punish it?

- Did I remember that this body is the dwelling place of the Breath-Giver?

This is not a checklist.

It is a conversation with your own nephesh.

A returning to the dust-and-breath reality of who you are.

MAY YOU BLESS WHAT THE WORLD TAUGHT YOU TO SHAME.

MAY YOUR MEALS BE MERCY, NOT MEASUREMENT.

MAY YOUR FEET FIND JOY, NOT JUDGMENT.

MAY YOUR SLEEP BE SAFE, YOUR HUNGER HOLY,

AND YOUR BODY A TEMPLE NOT OF STRIVING,

BUT OF SURRENDER.

YOU ARE NOT A MACHINE OR A PROBLEM TO FIX.

YOU ARE A LIVING SOUL—BREATH AND DUST,

FORMED IN LOVE, SUSTAINED BY GRACE,

AND CALLED TO WHOLENESS.

13

HEALING IN THE FIELD

They will rebuild the ancient ruins and restore the places long devastated;
they will renew the ruined cities that have been devastated for generations.

ISAIAH 61:4

HE NEVER MADE HEADLINES.

Never built a platform.

But everywhere he went, people became less alone.

He trained as a physician, but even then it was clear—his work wasn't about medicine alone. It was about showing up. About staying in the places most people leave.

For a season he practiced in the margins of an American city, offering care in a neighborhood where hope had long been evicted. Then he crossed the ocean, learning new languages, tending new wounds. He served in quiet clinics, in countries unfamiliar to most, caring for patients who had no advocate but him.

He stayed. Through language barriers. Through under-resourced systems.

Through pandemics and power outages. Through long seasons of isolation.

He stayed when others would have left.

But the field takes a toll.

There were no medals. No miraculous turnarounds.

Only the slow erosion that comes from loving deeply in hard places.

Eventually he returned. He came home in fatigue, not in failure.

The calling had not changed, but he had.

He came home not to quit but to rest.

To recover what had frayed.

To remember the feel of wholeness in his own breath and bones.

This, too, is healing in the field.

It isn't measured by outcomes or heroics. It's found in the courage to receive what you've offered: presence, kindness, care, restoration.

Even the healer needs to be healed.

THE FIELD: WHERE WHOLENESS MEETS FRACTURE

The field is not always a place.

It's wherever your soul intersects with sustained human need. The space where your vocation, your compassion, and your calling stretch you to the edge—and often beyond.

Sometimes it's a clinic. Sometimes a classroom, a hospital ward, a sanctuary, a living room, a family in freefall. Sometimes it's the quiet exhaustion of holding more than your soul was made to carry.

Scripture never promises ease for those sent into the field. But again and again, it shows us this: God meets people there—in the wilderness with Israel, in the villages where Jesus sent out the seventy-two, and in the cities where Paul proclaimed the gospel.

The field is where compassion costs something. Where simply being there feels insufficient. Where hope comes slowly, if at all. And yet it's often where healing takes root—not always in the patient or the system but in the one who finally learns to receive what they've spent a lifetime giving.

The field spills across professions and spaces: hospitals, kitchens, courtrooms, pulpits, counseling chairs. It's where medicine meets ministry, where service blurs into sacrifice, and where healing is most desperately needed—but also most easily lost.

You may not be able to leave the field. You may not be able to fix what's broken.

But you can remain whole within it.

JESUS IN THE FIELD

Scripture does not romanticize the field. It's dusty. Crowded. Fatiguing. It's where needs outnumber resources, where miracles are asked for with empty hands.

And yet that's where Jesus goes.

He doesn't stay in sanctuaries. He walks among the sick, the grieving, the hungry. He teaches from boats, touches lepers, listens to women long dismissed, bends low in the dust beside the guilty and the afraid.

When the disciples return from their own fieldwork, exhausted, He doesn't shame their weariness. He says, "Come away ... and rest" (Mark 6:31). But even then the crowds find them—and still, Jesus has compassion. He feeds five thousand. He breaks bread in the wilderness.

Jesus doesn't rush.

He doesn't flinch.

He stays whole, even when surrounded by fragmentation.

And this matters—because it means that wholeness is possible within the field. Not just after the work is done but while it's still unfolding.

Jesus shows us that being poured out does not require being emptied. That simply showing up can be healing, even when solutions are beyond reach. That the healer, too, is worthy of rest.

WHEN THE HEALER NEEDS HEALING

Clinical medicine is a deeply rewarding—but deeply taxing—calling. And I use that word intentionally. You don't just clock in. You carry it with you.

Burnout. Compassion fatigue. Emotional exhaustion. These aren't just buzzwords or abstract concepts. They're lived realities—epidemic in scope, especially in primary care. As one attending told me early on, "There are way easier ways to make money."

After ten years of practicing in a rural community, I began to feel what I had once only studied. What research described with clinical distance, I now felt in my own soul—the slow depletion, the fragmentation of presence, the growing gap between what I offered others and what I had left for myself.

I felt a call for restoration. But I didn't know what it needed to look like.

Then a trusted friend—a local pastor—reached out. He said he felt prompted to invite me on a trip to The Refuge, a retreat in the remote town of Hyattville, Wyoming. No cell phones. Long days of fly fishing. Stillness. A place for servants to be served.

My wife, ever perceptive and gracious, insisted I go. "You need this," she said. "You deserve it."

So I went—with no expectations, just a quiet ache I couldn't articulate.

After a few days of rest, reflection, and marginally successful fly fishing, something in me softened. Around a communal table one night, I found myself sharing what I had never quite put into words: That holding sacred space every day—bearing witness to marriages dissolving, cancer being named, anxiety mounting, hope slipping—takes a toll. That while I had learned to compartmentalize, there was still a spiritual cost to being present in so much suffering.

No matter how strong your walls, the burden seeps in.

The healer's soul frays.

The next day, during a prayer service called "Cowboy Communion," the Spirit arrived—not gently but like a long-withheld storm.

He met me with kindness and clarity. I hadn't come just to unplug. I had come to heal.

Ten years of unspoken sorrow, spiritual fatigue, and hidden scarring came to the surface. I wept. I laid it down. I gave it back.

And I heard Him whisper—firm and unmistakable: *You were never meant to carry this alone.*

That moment reoriented everything.

I began to understand—personally—what I'd told others so many times: That vocation is worship. That we are not meant to carry what only God can hold.

He is faithful to restore the soul of the healer too.

Since then, I've prayed this often: *Lord, I thank you for entrusting me with your love for others.*
I lay these burdens at your feet.
I release what I cannot fix.
I surrender what I cannot carry.
Heal what I cannot heal.
Let me walk freely again in your breath.

And in moments that beg for re-centering throughout the day, just this:

Lord, I give you what I cannot carry.

THE SACRED WEIGHT OF THE WORK

The field is not just emotional terrain. It's theological.

To labor in places of pain is to live in the unresolved tension of the already and not yet—the desire to heal and the reality that healing doesn't always come.

It is to serve with strength but meet the limits of what one soul can hold.

It is to ask the questions doctrine alone can't answer:

Why does healing come to some but not to others?

How do I remain present when I feel numb?

Where is God when the system stays broken?

These are not signs of weak faith. They are the reality of staying with eyes open in hard places.

And Scripture does not look away from them. It gives us a Savior who walked straight into them.

This is the promise of Isaiah 61: That those who have been restored will become restorers. Not by outcomes. Not by power. By presence. "They will rebuild the ancient ruins and restore the places long devastated" (Isaiah 61:4).

This isn't the work of heroism. It's the work of wholeness.

Of showing up, soul intact, and laying one brick of hope at a time. You may never see the full rebuilding.

But your presence is part of the restoration.

You carry not just your training, your skill, or your compassion— but the very breath of the One who stepped into the field before you.

PRACTICES OF REMAINING WHOLE ON THE FRONT LINES

Healing in the field doesn't just require skill. It requires soul.

And soul—nephesh—cannot be fabricated in a hurry. It must be tended, guarded, breathed into, especially in spaces of urgency and relentless need.

Remaining whole doesn't mean becoming invincible.

It means choosing to live as a living soul, even when everything around you tempts you to go numb.

Here are a few sustaining rhythms:

BOUNDARIES AS A GIFT, NOT A WALL

Boundaries are not selfish—they are sacred. They protect what is holy in you so that it can still be offered in love. They remind you that your identity rests in God—not in output or limitless availability.

Jesus often withdrew from crowds to preserve the nephesh needed to sustain the mission.

Wholeness doesn't require isolation. But it does require wisdom to say: This far. No further. Not today.

BREATH AND MARGIN AMID URGENCY

The field thrives on adrenaline, on efficiency, on speed. But the nephesh thrives on breath.

Create small margins of pause between tasks, between patients, between decisions. A hand on your chest. A whispered prayer in the hallway. A silent "Lord, I'm still here" before the next thing begins.

These are not wasted moments. They are the scaffolding of soul survival.

SEEING INDIVIDUALS, NOT OUTCOMES

When burnout creeps in, people become problems. Names become numbers. Faces blur. Outcomes dominate.

Wholeness in the field asks us to slow just enough to see—to remember that each person is a life to honor, not a task to complete.

Presence matters more than productivity.

Because no one ever healed from being rushed through.

LETTING THE SPIRIT INTERRUPT EFFICIENCY

You will be tempted to push, to power through, to ignore the tug. But sometimes the Spirit speaks loudest in the interruption.

The Spirit may nudge you to pause.

To ask one more question.

To sit for thirty extra seconds.

To let someone cry instead of rushing toward a solution.

Efficiency may win the moment. But presence can save the soul.

Healing in the field means you don't lose your soul while tending to others' wounds. It means choosing to remain a living nephesh in a place that doesn't always make space for it. It means letting God restore you—even as you pour out.

WHEN THE FIELD WOUNDS YOU

Sometimes, despite every rhythm, every prayer, every boundary you set, the field still gets to you. The healer becomes the hurting. The caregiver feels numb. The one who has held space for so many feels like there's no space left for themselves.

This isn't failure.

It's human.

To work in the field—especially over years or decades—is to expose your nephesh to fracture. It may happen so slowly you don't even notice, until one day you realize you can't feel what you used to. You snap when you didn't mean to. You dread the work that once felt sacred. Or worse—you feel nothing at all.

This is the hidden cost of caregiving.

The toll that doesn't always show up in the data but settles somewhere deep in the soul.

MORAL INJURY, BURNOUT, AND THE LIMITS OF ENDURANCE

Burnout isn't just exhaustion—it's grief.

Grief that you had to keep going when something inside you had already gone quiet.

Moral injury adds another layer—when you're forced to act against your values, to navigate systems that harm the people you want to help. You watch the fracture unfold—and feel powerless to stop it.

These aren't just psychological wounds.

They're spiritual ones.

They strike at the heart of what it means to live as a soul in a broken world.

A THEOLOGY OF LAMENT AND DUST

The field has always worn down the faithful. Even prophets collapsed.

Elijah, after confronting evil with divine fire, fled into the wilderness and asked to die. Ezekiel saw a vision of dry bones scattered in a valley. The psalmist cried out from a crushed and disquieted soul: "My tears have been my food day and night.... Why are you cast down, O my soul [nephesh]?" (Psalm 42:3, 5 ESV).

These laments were received, not rebuked.

God does not ask His servants to be invulnerable. He asks them to be honest. And when they fall, He does not shame them.

He brings food.

He brings water.

He brings His presence.

When the field wounds you, you do not need to hide.

You are not broken beyond repair.

The Breath-Giver is near to the crushed in spirit.

And He will restore you—not through shame but through rest.

A THIN PLACE: WHERE HEAVEN MEETS THE FIELD

There is a small, free medical clinic I serve in monthly. No high-end technology. No polished waiting rooms. Just a kaleidoscope of volunteers—doctors, nurses, students, scribes—offering their time freely.

It is, quite literally, a gathering of every tribe, tongue, and nation.

And it never fails to restore me.

Our patients reflect that same diversity—migrant workers, local families, people carrying hardship and resilience. Their needs are simple: presence, attention, care.

And in giving that care, we receive something ourselves.

The clinic is a thin place—where heaven and earth draw close. It's not glamorous, but it reorients me. In a fragmented world, it reminds me: Healing is not transactional.

It is relational.

Communal.

Sacramental.

Here, healing is mutual.

As we care for others, we are cared for.

As we offer presence, we are reminded of God's.

Boundaries matter. Margin matters. But I have found that so does pouring out—when it's done not for status or survival but for love. This is where the kingdom breaks through.

It is Eden, glimpsed again.

THE FIELD IS WHERE THE KINGDOM BREAKS IN

You are not just surviving the field.

You are rebuilding it—with your presence, with your breath, with the quiet faithfulness of showing up whole. Isaiah 61 begins with grief—but it ends with this:

> They will be called oaks of righteousness,
>> a planting of the LORD
>> for the display of his splendor.
> They will rebuild the ancient ruins
>> and restore the places long devastated.

(ISAIAH 61:3-4)

This is the kingdom: not power or perfection but dust-and-breath people becoming restorers—because they've been restored.

You may never see the full rebuilding.

You may never know what fruit your presence bore.

But make no mistake: Wholeness is never wasted.

Every time you breathe when the world demands hurry—

every time you see a person instead of a problem—

every time you pray in exhaustion or step away to rest—

you are carrying Eden into the wastelands.

You are not just tending the broken.

You are participating in the healing of the world.

Not through outcomes.

Through faithfulness.

Through breath.

Through wholeness that refuses to collapse.

This is the witness of the living nephesh:

To carry the Breath-Giver's presence into the places where breath has run thin.

To remember that the healer is also being healed.

And to know the field is not the end of the story—it's where the kingdom rises.

Pause here.

Breathe in: *Restore my soul, O Breath-Giver.*

Breathe out: *I give you what I cannot carry.*

You are not called to hold it all.

You are called to be whole.

Every breath of rest, every boundary honored, every quiet prayer in the field is worship.

The Breath-Giver does not ask for invincibility—only faithfulness.

Let your work be offering.

Let your rest be offering.

And trust Him to carry what you cannot.

REFLECTION: A BREATH FOR THE WEARY HEALER

Find a quiet space.

Unclench your jaw.

Feel the rise and fall of your breath.

You are not here to fix.

You are here to be.

Let these questions come gently.

Don't force answers. Just listen.

1. WHAT HAVE YOU BEEN CARRYING?

    What burdens have made their home in you?

    Whose pain have you held? Whose needs have stretched you thin?

    Are there stories still clinging to your skin—names, faces, outcomes unresolved?

    Let them surface.

    Not to be solved but to be seen.

2. WHERE ARE YOU RUNNING ON EMPTY?

Where have you been showing up without anything left to offer?

Where does your presence feel more like performance than peace?

Name the places you've gone numb.

Let yourself grieve what you've lost.

3. WHERE DO YOU NEED TO REST?

Rest—not avoidance, not indulgence, but holy pause.

Where does your body ache for margin?

Where does your spirit long for breath?

What would it look like to step away—not in failure but in faith?

4. WHERE MIGHT THE SPIRIT BE NUDGING YOU TO STAY?

Where have you been tempted to shut down? To power through? To close your heart to protect your soul?

Is the Spirit inviting you to remain—not as a martyr but as a whole person? Not in burnout but in breath?

5. WHAT WOULD IT MEAN TO LET GOD CARRY
   WHAT YOU CANNOT?

   What do you need to release today?

   What are you not responsible for?

MAY YOU FIND REST IN THE ONE WHO CARRIES WHAT YOU
CANNOT, OFFERS STRENGTH FOR WHAT REMAINS, AND
PROVIDES PEACE FOR ALL THAT LIES BEYOND YOU.

14

WHOLENESS AND WITNESS

"As the Father has sent me, I am sending you." And with that he breathed on them and said, "Receive the Holy Spirit."

JOHN 20:21-22

SHE CAME ONCE A YEAR.

A routine physical. Nothing urgent, nothing requested. Just an annual review of labs and screenings. She rarely needed anything in between.

She took care of her body—moved regularly, ate mindfully, tended her health with quiet discipline. But it was not her fitness that stayed with you. It was her presence.

Every time she walked through our doors, the atmosphere shifted—subtly, unmistakably. She carried peace like it was sewn into her breath. She hugged every member of the staff—not performatively but tenderly.

Calm. Grounded. Radiant.

At the end of each visit, without fail, she paused. Placed her hand on my shoulder. And she prayed. Not just for her health. Not for outcomes or solutions. She prayed for me. For my family. For my staff. For the work of our hands.

It wasn't long. It wasn't loud.

But it was always holy.

When she left, something lingered. Not because she tried to leave a mark—but because she was whole.

And wholeness, when carried gently, has a gravity all its own.

THE BREATH WE CARRY

The story began with breath. In the beginning God formed humanity from dust and breathed His Spirit into the clay. And the man became a living nephesh—a whole, animated, embodied soul. Not just a body. Not just a spirit. And when that soul fractured—when shame entered and communion was lost—everything scattered: presence, purpose, identity, rest. What was once whole became divided. But God was not content to let it stay that way.

He sent prophets. He made covenants. He gave His people rhythms to remember who they were. And in time, He Himself came. Jesus walked among us—not only to teach or to heal but to reunite what had been separated.

And on the other side of death, on the first evening of resurrection, He did something that should stop us in our tracks: "He breathed on them and said, 'Receive the Holy Spirit'" (John 20:22).

It's the only place in the New Testament where this Greek verb— *enephysēsen*—appears. Its only other biblical usage is in the Septuagint, where it describes the creation of Adam. This is not coincidence.

It was restoration. The same breath that animated the dust in Eden was given again—not just to make humanity but to remake it.

And as if this miraculous gesture were not enough, Jesus had more to say. He wished for healing not to stop with his disciples: "As the Father has sent me, I am sending you" (John 20:21). To be a living nephesh is not just to be healed. It is to be breathed upon—and then sent.

This is witness: not performance but participation. Not striving but Spirit-sent presence.

You are not sent because you are perfect.

You are sent because you are whole.

THE COST OF WITNESS

Witness isn't a spotlight, a microphone, a campaign, or a brand. It is the shape of a life made whole. You don't have to force it. Witness unfolds through how you live. It is what people see when someone breathes differently in a world that is always holding its breath.

It's the teacher who creates calm in a chaotic classroom. The nurse who stops typing and looks into the patient's eyes. The barista who remembers your name. The mother who breaks the generational script. The husband who listens without fixing. The coworker who refuses to gossip. The leader who chooses integrity over image. The patient who bears chronic pain with grace instead of bitterness.

> Witness is not what you say in a single moment. It is what your presence says over time. It's not loud. It's not flawless.

But it is unmistakably whole.

And wholeness shines—but it also unsettles.

Living as a whole person in a fragmented world is not always welcomed. Sometimes it's misunderstood. Sometimes resisted. Sometimes lonely. Because witness doesn't always look like victory. Sometimes it looks like presence that's ignored. Kindness that's questioned. Boundaries mistaken for coldness. Silence read as passivity.

And when you begin living nephesh—rooted, healed, no longer striving—you may find that others can't always meet you there.

You're not reactive enough to fuel outrage, not cynical enough to fit the crowd.

You're not productive enough for the grind, not self-promoting enough to play the game.

You may feel the urge to shrink. To explain. To prove.

You may wonder if something's wrong with you.

But there's not. You're simply breathing a different air now.

This is the cost of witness: not just persecution but the quiet ache of being out of sync with a world that is accustomed to fracture, a world numbed to hurry, distrust, and performance.

Even Jesus was misunderstood. Even He withdrew. Even He was weary. But He never stopped breathing peace into the places He entered.

And neither should you. Or I.

You've been breathed upon. You walk by a different rhythm now.

Even when no one sees it, it matters.

Because this is who you are now—whole, steady, sent.

OUTPOURING WHOLENESS IN DAILY LIFE

Not all witness wears a collar.

Not all callings are loud.

It's the parent who starts her morning not with a productivity list but with a whispered prayer: *Lord, let me be gentle today*. She doesn't parent perfectly, but her kids know her voice is a safe place. And when she messes up, she circles back. She names grace out loud. Her children are learning repentance not from lectures but from her life.

The coworker—not the most efficient on the team but the one people come to when they're breaking. He listens without glancing at the clock. He doesn't fix every problem but somehow, with his presence, makes the room feel lighter. Before meetings he breathes a silent prayer: *Let me be a calm place today.*

The churchgoer who sits in the back row. Never teaches. Never leads. But every Sunday she finds someone who looks alone—and sits beside them. She remembers names. She sees tears. Before she leaves, she scans the room and prays for every face she sees. She doesn't speak often, but her presence speaks for her.

The neighbor who waves at the same three families every evening on his walk. He checks the sky before he leaves and whispers a blessing for his street. He brings in the widow's trash bins without fanfare. Keeps extra lawn chairs in the garage, just in case someone needs to sit and talk. He doesn't quote Scripture. He lives it.

The patient in the waiting room who is still sick. Still struggling. Still in the valley. But when someone new sits down beside her, she turns and smiles first. She's the one who says: "I've been there. You're not alone." She is still waiting for her own healing. But in the meantime, she brings peace to the chairs around her.

These aren't grand gestures. They're not platformed, public, or polished.

They are the quiet overflow of whole lives.

They are the witness of the breathed-upon—people whose integration, not performance, becomes a healing presence.

NEPHESH LIVING

Pause here.

Breathe in: *I am still a living soul.*

Breathe out: *Send me with your presence.*

You do not carry wholeness for yourself alone.

Every word you speak, every silence you keep, every step you take can become witness.

Your presence—steady, imperfect, Spirit breathed—makes space for others to breathe too.

REFLECTION: A BREATH BEFORE YOU GO

You've walked through a long journey.

Not toward perfection—but toward presence.

Not toward having all the answers—but toward knowing the One who breathes life into dust.

Before you move on, pause.

Make space to receive what the Spirit is still whispering.

1. WHERE HAVE YOU TASTED WHOLENESS LATELY?

    A conversation that softened you?

    A moment where you felt present, even in pain?

    A breath that felt like enough?

    Let it rise. Give thanks for it.

2. WHERE ARE YOU STILL TEMPTED TO FRAGMENT?

    Where do you still perform? Hide? Push through?

    What do you find hardest to bring your full self into?

    Name it. Gently. Without shame.

3. WHERE MIGHT YOUR PRESENCE BECOME WITNESS?

Is there someone, some place, some ordinary rhythm that might be transformed not by your strength but by your steadiness?

Ask the Spirit to breathe there.

4. WHERE DO YOU STILL NEED BREATH YOURSELF?

You do not have to earn rest.

You do not have to carry everyone.

What might it mean to let God minister to you, even as you are sent?

Open your hands.

Receive the breath again.

YOU'VE COME A LONG WAY—NOT TO PERFECTION OR CONTROL BUT FROM SCATTERED TO GATHERED, FROM FRAGMENTED TO RESTORED, FROM SURVIVING TO WHOLE. YOU HAVE RECEIVED THE BREATH OF GOD AGAIN— NOT ONCE LONG AGO, BUT NOW. TODAY.

AND THAT BREATH IS NOT JUST FOR YOUR HEALING. IT IS FOR THE WORLD.

WHOLENESS IS NOT A DESTINATION BUT A WITNESS.

YOU ARE NOT SENT TO SAVE THE WORLD BUT TO LIVE AS
SOMEONE WHO HAS BEEN SAVED.

TO WALK LIKE SOMEONE WHO HAS BEEN SEEN.

TO SPEAK LIKE SOMEONE WHO HAS BEEN LOVED.

TO REST LIKE SOMEONE WHO TRUSTS THE RHYTHM OF GRACE.

WHEREVER YOU GO, THE BREATH-GIVER GOES WITH YOU.
AND EVERY ROOM YOU ENTER BECOMES A PLACE OF
POSSIBILITY. NOT BECAUSE YOU CARRY THE ANSWER BUT
BECAUSE YOU CARRY THE PRESENCE.

YOU ARE NOT RESPONSIBLE FOR EVERYONE ELSE'S HEALING.
BUT YOUR WHOLENESS MAKES SPACE FOR THEIRS.

YOU ARE NOT THE SOURCE OF BREATH; YOU FOLLOW THE ONE
WHO FIRST BREATHED INTO DUST—AND STILL DOES.

BUT YOU ARE A LIVING SOUL.

MAY YOUR LIFE BEAR WITNESS TO THE GOD WHO MAKES
ALL THINGS WHOLE.

EPILOGUE

A GENESIS MOMENT

I FOUND THE FOLLOWING EMAIL tucked away in my archives while finishing the final edits of this book. I hadn't read it since the time I wrote it.

It was written in May 2020, in the early months of the pandemic—a time when everything felt uncertain and heavy. I had just listened to Strahan Coleman speak about the Hebrew concept of nephesh in one of his brilliant online prayer schools, and something cracked open in me. I didn't have language for it then, but I knew something had shifted.

What you'll read below is raw and unpolished. It wasn't written with publication in mind—just a late-night attempt to put words around the ache and realization that had been growing inside me for years.

Looking back now, I can see that this was the moment the roots of *Living Nephesh* first pressed toward the surface.

I'm sharing it here not because it's profound but because it's honest. It captures a before-and-after in my own journey—a moment of clarity I'll never forget. I offer it with gratitude to Strahan and in the hope that someone else might see their own story in mine.

ORIGINALLY WRITTEN TO STRAHAN COLEMAN, MAY 2020
—shared here with deep gratitude.

Last night you described something so profound that it stopped me in my tracks. It captured what I see in medical practice every day—and though I've always brought my faith into my work and viewed my office as a kind of mission field, I realize now that I've been missing something until last night.

This idea of nephesh is deep, man.

I've been in practice for about eight years. I've seen God heal people in all kinds of ways—mental, emotional, physical—from depression, anxiety, panic disorder, and substance dependence, to diabetes, cancer, and autoimmune conditions. Sometimes medicine helps dramatically. Sometimes it's a spiritual issue that needs attention. Sometimes it's an unhealthy relationship that's breaking the body open from the inside out.

Whatever the nuanced reasons may be, I see God use one, some, or all of these tools to bring healing. And the formula is never the same. Despite what the really "churchy" voices might say, it often can't be boiled down to a purely spiritual plane—or chalked up to someone "not having enough faith." Those four words can be some of the most destructive in the Christian vocabulary, and my heart laments how many have been turned away from the church because of them.

The point of all this rambling is: I realize now that I've unknowingly fallen into a kind of functional Gnosticism. I've treated the spiritual as something transcendent, separate from the body—and though I've told myself I was approaching patients holistically (addressing exercise, nutrition, faith, and sometimes medication), I was doing it in a disjointed way.

This idea of nephesh—of the whole, living soul—has been an "aha" moment for me. A light turned on. It explains how God can use lifestyle change, medicine, spiritual awakening, relational restoration—all of it—in harmony. Not as separate parts, but as responses to a single, sacred essence.

I think of one person who prays through mental health crises and finds healing as she draws nearer to God, never needing medication.

I think of another who, lost in a dense, unshakable depression, finally hears God's voice again after starting an antidepressant.

I think of a man who conquers anxiety through clean eating and regular movement, his body finding rhythm and his mind following.

Each of these stories points back to the same truth: it's all connected. One central essence. One nephesh.

What I see day in and day out affirms the reality and practical importance of this vision. I hope I've communicated that clearly enough—because for me, this shift in perspective hasn't just been a theological nuance. It's been life-changing. Personally, professionally, and spiritually.

It's changing how I practice medicine. It's affirming my faith. And it's drawing me closer to understanding who our Creator really is—and how He created us to live.

God bless you, my friend.

And thank you.

—PAYTON

APPENDIX A

A SPIRITUAL INVENTORY FOR THE LIVING SOUL

DISCERNING WHERE YOU ARE SO YOU CAN RETURN TO WHO YOU ARE

THIS INVENTORY IS A COMPANION to chapter 6.

It is not a diagnostic tool—it's a mirror. A way to gently notice where disintegration may be quietly at work within your nephesh.

Move slowly. Breathe deeply. Let the Spirit guide you—not into shame but into clarity and restoration. Use it in moments of drift, depletion, or discernment. Let it help you listen.

1. THE BREATH

Your connection with God's presence and your own interior life.

- When was the last time I experienced God's nearness?

- Do I find myself praying out of connection—or just out of crisis or obligation?

- What do I believe about God's posture toward me right now?

- When was the last time I felt awe, wonder, or deep peace?

- Am I making room for stillness, silence, or Sabbath in any form?

- Do I feel like I'm holding my spiritual breath, trying to earn air?

- Am I numbing spiritual hunger with noise, productivity, or distraction?

2. THE BODY

Your embodied rhythms of health, rest, and physical integration.

- How is my sleep—deep and restorative, or restless and interrupted?

- How am I feeding myself—hurriedly, restrictively, thoughtfully, mindlessly?

- Do I feel at home in my body, or do I relate to it with frustration or neglect?

- Have I moved my body this week in ways that felt joyful or grounding?

- What is my body trying to tell me lately (fatigue, headaches, irritability, tension)?

- Am I overriding my limits in the name of duty, guilt, or urgency?

- Do I honor my body as part of my worship or see it as something to control or ignore?

3. BELONGING

Your experience of relational safety, connection, and vulnerability.

- Who knows what I'm really going through right now?

- Do I feel seen and safe in my closest relationships—or tolerated, useful, invisible?

- Am I carrying unspoken resentment or unmet need in any key relationship?

- Have I withdrawn emotionally from people I once trusted?

- Do I feel the need to hide my weakness, mask my emotions, or manage others' perceptions?

- Where have I felt the joy of being known recently?

- Have I been present and tender with those I love—or reactive, guarded, or absent?

4. BECOMING

Your sense of purpose, direction, identity, and soul alignment.

- What voices are shaping my identity right now—truthful or toxic?

- Am I living from a place of rooted calling or reactive pressure?

- Is my work (paid or unpaid) still connected to my deepest "why"?

- What false scripts or inherited roles am I still performing?

- Where have I said yes when I should have said no?

- What part of me is aching for permission to change—or to rest?

- Who am I becoming as a result of my current habits, relationships, and inner dialogue?

5. BLESSING

Receiving, speaking, and naming sacred worth.

- When was the last time I received a word of blessing—from God or from someone else?

- Have I allowed myself to believe that I am loved, not just useful?

- What does God say is true about me right now?

- When I imagine Jesus looking at me, what expression is on His face?

- Have I ever spoken blessing aloud over someone in my household or circle?

- Am I more comfortable serving others than letting them care for me?

- Where might I be invited to speak blessing—not correction—over myself?

FINAL REFLECTION: SOUL LISTENING

Choose one question from each section that stirred you most. Gently name what came up. Then ask:

- What is the Spirit revealing to me—not to condemn but to restore?

- Is there a rhythm I've lost that I want to recover?

- Where do I feel invited—not to overhaul my life but to take one breath-aligned step?

APPENDIX B

PRACTICING WHOLENESS IN
SMALL WAYS

A CATALOG OF GENTLE INVITATIONS FOR THE LIVING SOUL

THIS CATALOG FLOWS from chapter 7's invitation to begin again in small, faithful ways.

Each practice corresponds to one of the five dimensions of living nephesh—breath, body, belonging, becoming, and blessing.

These are not tasks to achieve but gentle invitations to return. Let one stir something in you. Then begin there.

You might

- choose one practice each week and reflect on how it shapes your awareness.

- select one from each category and create a day of integrated rest.

Return to this catalog when you feel fragmented, and begin again.

BREATH—LEARNING TO RECEIVE

Practices that center the soul through breath, silence, and presence.

- Begin the day with three slow breaths before checking your phone.

- Set a timer to pause and breathe at noon, anchoring your day.

- Practice exhaling longer than you inhale.

- Try a breath prayer: *You are the vine, Lord.* (Inhale). *Help me to abide.* (Exhale).

- Sit in silence for two minutes with a candle, letting your breath be your prayer.

- Recite Psalm 23 slowly, one verse per breath cycle.

- Step outside and take five deep breaths in the fresh air.

- Close your eyes and count ten slow breaths during transitions.

- Breathe through a difficult emotion instead of reacting to it.

- Let your breathing pace you while doing a chore—folding laundry, washing dishes.

BODY—HONORING THE DUST

Practices that reconnect you with your physical self as sacred.

- Stretch in the morning for five minutes before getting dressed.

- Take a walk without headphones. Listen to the world around you.

- Drink a full glass of water slowly, with gratitude.

- Eat one meal without screens, noise, or multitasking.

- Thank God for your body exactly as it is right now.

- Lay flat on the floor for ten minutes without needing to "do" anything.

- Step outside barefoot and feel the ground beneath you.

- Massage your hands or feet as an act of care, not critique.

- Prepare a meal from scratch and notice the textures, smells, and colors.

- Practice good sleep hygiene for one week: same bedtime, no screens, a gentle wind-down.

- Engage in vigorous movement—running, lifting, dancing, or working—while praying with your breath in gratitude: *I offer this strength to you.*

- Choose one activity you normally do to burn calories—and instead do it to glorify God with your body.

- Let your heartbeat become a rhythm of praise. Name God's goodness with every step.

- During exercise, thank God aloud for what your body can do—its movement, breath, endurance, and strength.

BELONGING—DWELLING WITH OTHERS

Practices that deepen connection and embody presence.

- Send a blessing text to someone who wouldn't expect it.

- Ask a loved one, "How's your soul?" instead of "How are you?"

- Share a meal with someone—and resist the urge to fill every silence.

- Make eye contact and offer a smile to a stranger.

- Let someone help you with something you usually do alone.

- Offer a sincere apology, even for something small.

- Sit with a friend in silence when words aren't needed.

- Write a short note to someone who once shaped your life.

- Invite someone over with no agenda but being together.

- Practice listening without interrupting or rehearsing your reply.

BECOMING—MOVING TOWARD WHAT MATTERS

Practices that help you notice your purpose and shape your soul.

- Reread a Scripture or prayer that once stirred something in you.

- Make a short list of three things that bring you life this season.

- Choose one task to do slowly and with care today.

- Reflect on this question: What do I feel drawn toward, and why?

- Speak aloud a hope you've been afraid to name.

- Journal for five minutes before bed: Where did I feel most alive today?

- Identify one area of misalignment in your life—and ask God about it.

- Take a tech Sabbath for a few hours, or a full day if possible.

- Ask, What am I becoming through the way I'm living?

- Revisit a dream you set down. Pray over whether it's time to pick it back up.

BLESSING–LIVING AS A VESSEL OF OVERFLOW

Practices that let grace pass through you and toward others.

- Speak aloud a word of blessing over your home.

- Bless someone in traffic or a public space instead of judging them.

- Pray for someone anonymously—and never tell them.

- Write a blessing for a friend's future and mail it, even without occasion.

- Gently bless your children or spouse as they sleep.

- Stand under the shower and say, "May I receive what I need to give today."

- Place your hand over your heart and speak a blessing over your past self.

- When you cook, bless those who will eat—even if it's just you.

- Ask God, "Who needs blessing through me today?" and follow the nudge.

- Give money away this week—not out of guilt but joy. Let it point someone toward wholeness.

- Pray over your budget: *God, how would you have me steward what I've been given?*

- Tithe not as a rule but as a rhythm of trust and gratitude.

- Support someone's dream—buy their book, fund their fundraiser, tip with abundance.

- Bless your enemies—not to change them but to change you.

APPENDIX C

CRAFTING A RULE OF LIFE FOR THE LIVING SOUL

A FRAMEWORK FOR INTENTIONAL, INTEGRATED WHOLENESS

THIS FRAMEWORK IS A COMPANION to chapter 8.

It offers space to begin shaping your own rule of life—one that reflects your season, your longings, and your call to abide.

Built around the five dimensions of wholeness, this rule is not about control. It is about consent. A quiet yes to living as a whole soul before God.

BEFORE YOU BEGIN: REFLECT

Take a few moments to ground yourself before creating your rule.

- Where am I feeling most whole right now?

- Where do I feel scattered, weary, or fragmented?

- What has helped me feel most alive or aligned in recent weeks?

- What do I long for more of in my life? What do I long to release?

Your answers don't need to be profound—just honest.

BREATH—REST, SILENCE, AND RECEIVING

"I regularly pause to receive rather than strive."
Practices to consider:

- Begin each morning with a breath prayer or silence.

- Take one digital-free hour each evening.

- Protect one full Sabbath day per week.

- End each day with Examen or gratitude journaling.

- Use transitions (car rides, sink time, elevators) as breath cues.

MY RHYTHM OF BREATH

BODY—EMBODIED CARE AND STRENGTH

"I will honor the dust with gentleness, strength, and stewardship."
Practices to consider:

- Move my body three to five times per week (walk, run, lift, dance, stretch).

- Exercise at least once a week with gratitude as worship.

- Nourish myself with at least one slow, attentive meal daily.

- Keep a consistent sleep rhythm (bedtime, wake time, wind-down).

- Name aloud one thing I appreciate about my body each day.

- Practice nutritional stewardship—eating foods that are as whole, nourishing, and unprocessed as your context allows, not out of perfectionism but as an act of honoring the body God formed from the earth.

MY RHYTHM OF BODY

BELONGING–PRESENCE WITH OTHERS
"I will make space to dwell meaningfully with others."
Practices to consider:

- Share a meal with others at least once a week.

- Reach out to one person intentionally each week (text, letter, call).

- Offer or receive help without judgment of self or others.

- Pray for others during everyday tasks (laundry, driving, dishes).

- Bless my children, spouse, or housemates daily—through words or presence.

MY RHYTHM OF BELONGING

BECOMING–PURPOSE AND GROWTH
"I will shape my days toward what matters most."
Practices to consider:

- Set aside daily time for Scripture, journaling, or reflection.

- Ask monthly: What am I becoming through the way I'm living?

- Schedule one creative or deeply engaging activity per week.

- Practice tech Sabbath—half day or full day, weekly or monthly.

- Make space regularly for dreaming and discernment.

MY RHYTHM OF BECOMING

BLESSING–LIVING FROM OVERFLOW

"I will let grace pass through me—spiritually, relationally, and materially."
Practices to consider:

- Tithe or give financially as a firstfruit rhythm.

- Budget prayerfully: "How would you have me steward this, Lord?"

- Contribute to a kingdom cause—missions, local ministry, or child sponsorship—as a rhythm of generosity, not guilt.

- Participate regularly in service that directly impacts the poor: volunteering at a soup kitchen, free medical clinic, or local thrift store as an act of presence and solidarity.

- Bless someone with my words every day.

- Speak a blessing over my own life each morning or night.

- Be quick to forgive, quick to offer mercy.

MY RHYTHM OF BLESSING

YOUR RULE OF LIFE: A LIVING FRAMEWORK

This rule is not static—it is a living document for a living soul. Revisit it each season. You might write a new one at the start of each quarter or review it gently when life shifts. Use this space to summarize the rhythms you want to hold in this moment:

My Rule of Life (summary):

BREATH: _____

BODY: _____

BELONGING: _____

BECOMING: _____

BLESSING: _____

Name the tone of this season (circle or underline):

GENTLE / REBUILDING / ROOTED / COURAGEOUS /

QUIET / PLAYFUL / FOCUSED / HEALING

APPENDIX D

THE FAMILY SOUL MAP

A REFLECTIVE PRACTICE FOR BECOMING WHOLE TOGETHER

THIS VISUAL REFLECTION grows out of chapter 10.

The Family Soul Map invites you to explore the relational tone, inherited patterns, and healing invitations present within your household—past or present.

It's not a tool for judgment. It's a practice of seeing clearly—so that, by grace, we can live differently and love more wholly.

> These commandments ... impress them on your children. Talk about
> them when you sit at home and when you walk along the road.
> (Deuteronomy 6:6–7)

STEP 1: OBSERVE THE RHYTHMS

REFLECT

- What are the daily rhythms that currently shape our home? (meals, tech use, Sabbath, sleep, connection)

- Where do we move in sync?

- Where do we move in isolation or hurry?

- What feels sacred in our week? What feels chaotic?

You might use a visual map, a family conversation, or quiet reflection to name these shared patterns.

STEP 2: TRACE THE FRACTURES

REFLECT

- Where are we most reactive as a family?

- What topics or behaviors consistently create disconnection?

- Are there old wounds—spoken or unspoken—that still shape our tone?

- What do we avoid naming, and why?

This step isn't about assigning blame but becoming aware of pain that hadn't yet been brought into the light. Wholeness begins with honesty.

STEP 3: NAME THE STRENGTHS

REFLECT

- What do we celebrate well?

- How do we make one another feel seen or loved?

- When have we experienced joy or unity recently?

- What's unique about how our family expresses care?

These are signs of grace—evidences of integration already at work. Name them. Rehearse them.

STEP 4: LISTEN FOR INVITATION

Ask as a family (or as an individual reflecting on your household):

- What might God be inviting us to shift, reclaim, or release?

- Which of the five Bs (breath, body, belonging, becoming, blessing) feel most alive in our home?

- Which feel neglected or fractured?

- What is one small, doable step we could take this week toward wholeness?

You might choose to:

- Institute a screen-free dinner or bedtime blessing.

- Set a weekly family Sabbath rhythm.

- Begin a short gratitude or prayer practice with your children.

- Apologize or reconcile where something has long been left unsaid.

STEP 5: CREATE A FAMILY RHYTHM STATEMENT (OPTIONAL)

Close the practice by writing a short, shared declaration or intention for this season.

EXAMPLE: "We are a household of breath and blessing. We choose presence over hurry, grace over perfection, and joy over resistance. We are learning to become whole—together."

APPENDIX E

WHY WORDS MATTER—*NEPHESH*, *PSYCHE*, *SARX*—AND THE LANGUAGE OF WHOLENESS

THIS APPENDIX EXPANDS on the theological thread in chapter 3.

It traces how the translation of *nephesh* into Greek terms like *psyche* and *soma* shaped Christian theology—and how that shift continues to impact how we see the body, the soul, and the meaning of wholeness.

If you've ever sensed a disconnect between what Scripture teaches and how we live, this may help name the root.

The biblical vision is not confused. But the languages we use—and sometimes our inherited theological frameworks—have introduced distortions.

At the heart of *Living Nephesh* is a claim: that the human person is not a divided collection of parts but a unified being—a living soul—formed by God from dust and breath. This is the vision offered in Genesis 2:7 and echoed in the life and teachings of Jesus. But some readers may ask, "If that's true, why does the New Testament use terms like *body, soul, spirit,* and *flesh*? Doesn't that suggest we are divided after all?"

It's a fair question—and it deserves a thoughtful response.

FROM HEBREW INTEGRATION TO GREEK CATEGORIZATION

The Old Testament, written in Hebrew, speaks of human beings in integrated terms. The word *nephesh* occurs over seven hundred times, and it refers not to a "soul" trapped inside a body but to the whole living person—a breathing, feeling, thinking, embodied life.[1] Nephesh bleeds. It hungers. It touches. It praises. It dies.

When the Hebrew Bible was translated into Greek (the Septuagint), translators had no exact equivalent for *nephesh*. They often used *psyche* (ψυχή), a Greek word that originally referred to life force or soul—but one shaped by centuries of Greek philosophy, particularly Plato's idea of the soul as eternal and superior to the body. The result? A shift in tone:

- *Nephesh* = whole person (earth + breath, indivisible)

- *Psyche* = soul or mind (often contrasted with body)

This shift didn't mean Scripture changed its anthropology—it meant the words used to convey that anthropology were now vulnerable to cultural reinterpretation.

WHAT ABOUT PAUL? *SARX, SOMA,* AND *SPIRIT*

In the New Testament, especially Paul's letters, we see a range of Greek terms used to describe the human person:

- *Soma* (σῶμα)—body, often neutral or even positive (e.g., "your bodies are temples")

---

1 Kenneth W. Peacock, "Translating the Word for 'Soul' in the Old Testament," The Bible Translator 27, no. 2 (April 1976): 219–26, https://translation.bible/wp-content/uploads/2024/06/peacock-1976-translating-the-word-for-soul-in-the-old-testament.pdf.

- *Psyche* (ψυχή)—soul/life, sometimes used similarly to *nephesh*, especially in the Gospels

- *Pneuma* (πνεῦμα)—spirit, frequently describing life aligned with God

- *Sarx* (σάρξ)—flesh, often used negatively to describe the self under sin's dominion

At first glance this seems like a fragmented anthropology. But Paul is not offering a metaphysical anatomy chart. He's using the vocabulary of his day to describe lived experience—especially the way sin disintegrates the human person and grace reintegrates it.

Paul's goal is not to divide the human into parts but to describe the tension between two ways of being human—a life lived "according to the flesh" (*sarx*) versus a life "according to the Spirit" (*pneuma*).

So while Paul uses distinct terms, he does so relationally, not onto-logically. His vision is still Hebraic at its core: God made us as whole beings. Sin fractures that wholeness. Christ restores it.[2]

JESUS, THE SHEMA, AND THE LAYERS OF PERSONHOOD

Even Jesus's words—"Love the Lord your God with all your heart, soul, mind, and strength" (Matthew 22:37)—are best read not as a checklist of parts but a poetic stacking of synonyms.[3] This is an interpretive pattern common in Hebrew literature: layering to emphasize totality.

Jesus is echoing the *Shema* (Deuteronomy 6:4–5), where *nephesh* means your whole self. His aim is not to divide but to deepen. You

---

2   N. T. Wright, *The Resurrection of the Son of God* (Fortress Press, 2003), esp. 141–44, 367–70.

3   R. T. France, *The Gospel of Matthew*, The New International Commentary on the New Testament (William B. Eerdmans Publishing Company, 2007), 849–52.

could paraphrase: "Love God with everything you are, every layer of your being, every breath, every act, every thought."

FROM FRAGMENTATION TO WHOLENESS

We live in the long shadow of dualism—Plato's hierarchy of soul over body, Descartes's vision of mind from flesh. But the biblical witness has always offered a different vision. In Genesis God breathes into dust, and the human becomes a nephesh—a living soul. In John 20:22 Jesus breathes again, and the disciples receive the Spirit. Dust and breath are rejoined. Wholeness is restored.

The words changed, but the story never did.

This is the story *Living Nephesh* seeks to reclaim. Not a rejection of the New Testament vocabulary but a recovery of the unified human vision that runs beneath it all.

ACKNOWLEDGMENTS

THIS BOOK WAS NEVER WRITTEN ALONE.

It was formed in conversation and quiet, in prayer and in pause.

It took shape in early mornings before the house stirred,

in exam rooms, late-night texts, unspoken knowing, and sacred friendship.

What follows is only a small naming of a much deeper gratitude.

TO CLORY–

Without you, this book could not exist.

Not simply because you made space for its writing, but because you made space for me—for my healing, for my returning.

My road back to wholeness—back to Eden, back to the Breath-Giver—began with you.

You are grace made visible.

You are the first witness of this journey, and always its heart.

TO BERKLEY, BRITTON, AND BECKETT–

You are my joy.

Not because of what you achieve but because of who you are.

Each of you carries a light that reminds me daily of God's goodness, nearness, and mercy.

May you grow strong in spirit, tender in love, and unshakably whole—living nephesh in a world aching for it.

TO MOM AND DAD—
For the foundation you gave me, and for the ways your love formed the soil of my becoming.

TO JO AND STEVE W.—
For showing me that family is never bound by blood alone.

For reminding me that the love of God is the strongest bond a soul can know.

For knowing me at my best and my worst—and choosing love, every time.

TO MY LIFE GROUP—
You are my people.

Your laughter, prayers, and presence have held me fast.

You walked with me not only as this book was written but as I became the kind of person who could write it.

TO TREVOR, BOBBY, ADAM C., JUSTIN, MICHAEL, JOSH, NICK, AND JACOB S.—
You believed in me when I could not.

You carried this dream with me, even when I wasn't sure it could bear fruit.

Your faithfulness is etched between every line.

TO WES, ALAN, JACOB R., GAVIN, AND DAVE S.—
You shaped me—in the field, in the fire, in the quiet moments where wisdom whispered and witness endured.

Your voices echo through these pages.

Thank you for being both mentors and brothers.

TO STRAHAN COLEMAN–

Your words reawakened my soul.

You reminded me that prayer is presence, that formation begins not with striving but with stillness.

This book was born in the ache your voice named.

TO TIM KELLER–

Though we never met, you taught me to see Jesus with clearer eyes.

Your mind, your heart, your vision opened paths I didn't know could be walked.

I count you among my teachers, and always will.

TO DORI HARRELL–

Your grace and careful eye not only refined these pages but reminded me that this vision was worthy of sharing—and that I was worthy to share it. This book is stronger, truer, and clearer because of you.

TO MARK KARIS–

You have captured beauty in form and texture.

TO EVERY UNNAMED SOUL WHOSE KINDNESS SHAPED THIS JOURNEY–

Thank you. Your fingerprints remain on these pages.

This is my work.

But it is not mine alone.

The witness is shared. The breath was borrowed.

And the glory belongs to the Giver of it all.

BIBLIOGRAPHY

American Psychiatric Association. *Diagnostic and Statistical Manual of Mental Disorders: DSM-5-TR.* 5th ed., text revision. American Psychiatric Publishing, 2022.

Balban, Muhammed Y., Melis Yilmaz Balban, David Spiegel, and Andrew D. Huberman. "Brief Structured Respiration Practices Enhance Mood and Reduce Physiological Arousal." *Cell Reports Medicine* 4, no. 2 (February 21, 2023): 100936. https://doi.org/10.1016/j.xcrm.2023.100936

Barr, James. *The Semantics of Biblical Language.* Oxford University Press, 1961.

BeDuhn, Jason. *Augustine's Manichaean Dilemma, Volume 2: Making a "Catholic" Self, 388–401 C.E.* University of Pennsylvania Press, Incorporated, 2013.

Bonhoeffer, Dietrich. *Life Together.* Translated by John W. Doberstein. San Francisco: Harper & Row, 1954.

Bowlby, John. *Attachment.* Vol. 1 of the Attachment and Loss series. Basic Books, 1969.

Buettner, Dan, and Suzanne Skemp. "Blue Zones: Lessons from the World's Longest Lived." *American Journal of Lifestyle Medicine* 10, no. 5 (2016): 318–21. https://doi.org/10.1177/1559827616637066.

Centers for Disease Control and Prevention. "Health Effects of Social Isolation and Loneliness." Last reviewed May 15, 2024. https://www.cdc.gov/social-connectedness/risk-factors/index.html.

Chang, Edward, Sanjay Basu, Benjamin Smith. "Care Fragmentation, Quality, and Costs Among Chronically Ill Patients." *American Journal of Managed Care*, May 2023. https://www.ajmc.com/view/care-fragmentation-quality-costs-among-chronically-ill-patients.

Cole, Steve W., et al. "Social Regulation of Gene Expression in Human Leukocytes." *Proceedings of the National Academy of Sciences* 104, no. 24 (2007): 10671–76. https://pubmed.ncbi.nlm.nih.gov/17854483/.

Descartes, René. *Meditations on First Philosophy.* Translated by John Cottingham. Cambridge: Cambridge University Press, 1996.

Felitti, Vincent J., Robert F. Anda, et al. "Relationship of Childhood Abuse and Household Dysfunction to Many of the Leading Causes of Death in Adults: The Adverse Childhood Experiences (ACE) Study." *American Journal of Preventive Medicine* 14, no. 4 (1998): 245–58. https://doi.org/10.1016/S0749-3797(98)00017-8.

Foucault, Michel. *The Birth of the Clinic: An Archaeology of Medical Perception.* Translated by A. M. Sheridan. New York: Vintage Books, 1994.

France, R. T. *The Gospel of Matthew.* The New International Commentary on the New Testament. William B. Eerdmans Publishing Company, 2007.

Frank, Arthur W. The Wounded Storyteller: Body, Illness, and Ethics. University of Chicago Press, 1995.

Grey, Sarah. "Friday Night Meatballs: How to Change Your Life with Pasta." *Serious Eats*. August 18, 2014. https://www.seriouseats. com/simpler-entertaining-friday-night-dinners-end-loneliness-how-to-build-community-after-having-kids.

Holt-Lunstad, Julianne, Timothy B. Smith, et al. "Loneliness and Social Isolation as Risk Factors for Mortality: A Meta-Analytic Review." *Perspectives on Psychological Science* 10, no. 2 (2015): 227–37. https://pubmed.ncbi.nlm.nih.gov/25910392.

Jee Young Joo. "Fragmented Care and Chronic Illness Patient Outcomes: A Systematic Review." *Nursing Open* 10, no. 6 (2023): 3460–73. https://doi.org/10.1002/nop2.1607.

Kelley, John M., Helen C. Kraft-Todd, et al. "The Influence of the Patient-Clinician Relationship on Healthcare Outcomes: A Systematic Review and Meta-Analysis of Randomized Controlled Trials." *PLOS ONE* 9, no. 4 (2014): e94207. https://doi.org/10.1371/journal.pone.0094207.

Koenig, Harold G. "Religion, Spirituality, and Health: The Research and Clinical Implications." *ISRN Psychiatry* (2012): 1–33. https://doi.org/10.5402/2012/278730.

Lee, Alyona G., Shielene B. Vargas, et al. "Exploring Plant-Based Diets and Mental Health Outcomes: A Systematic Review." *Cureus* 17, no. 8 (2025): e89846. https://doi.org/10.7759/cureus.89846.

Li, Shanshan, Meir J. Stampfer, et al. "Association of Religious Service Attendance with Mortality Among Women." *JAMA Internal*

Medicine 176, no. 6 (2016): 777–85. https://doi.org/10.1001/ jamainternmed.2016.1615.

Mackie, Tim, and the Bible Project. "What Is the Shema?' BibleProject. Accessed May 5, 2025. https://bibleproject.com/articles/ what-is-the-shema/.

Middleton, J. Richard. "Paul on the Soul: Not What You Might Think." *Creation to Eschaton* (blog). October 23, 2014. https://jrichardmiddleton. com/2014/10/23/paul-on-the-soul-not-what-you-might-think/.

Murthy, Vivek H. *Our Epidemic of Loneliness and Isolation: The U.S Surgeon General's Advisory on the Healing Effects of Social Connection and Community.* US Department of Health and Human Services 2023. https://www.hhs.gov/sites/default/files/surgeon-general-social-connection-advisory.pdf.

Peacock, Kenneth W. "Translating the Word for 'Soul' in the Old Testament." The Bible Translator 27, no. 2 (April 1976): 219–26. https://translation.bible/wp-content/uploads/2024/06/peacock-1976-translating-the-word-for-soul-in-the-old-testament.pdf.

Perry, Bruce D., and Maia Szalavitz. *The Boy Who Was Raised as a Dog: And Other Stories from a Child Psychiatrist's Notebook.* 3rd ed. Basic Books, 2021.

Pham, H. H., D. Schrag, A. S. O'Malley, B. Wu, and P. B. Bach. "Care Patterns in Medicare and Their Implications for Pay for Performance." *New England Journal of Medicine* 356, no. 11 (2007): 1130–39.

Plato. *Plato's Phaedo: A Translation of Plato's Phaedo with Introduction, Notes and Appendices.* Translated by R. S. Bluck. Routledge, 2000.

Porges, Stephen W. *The Polyvagal Theory: Neurophysiological Foundations of Emotions, Attachment, Communication, and Self-Regulation*. W. W. Norton & Company, 2011.

Porges, Stephen W. "The Polyvagal Theory: New Insights into Adaptive Reactions of the Autonomic Nervous System." *Cleveland Clinic Journal of Medicine* 76, no. S2 (2009): S86–S90. https://doi.org/10.3949/ccjm.76.s2.17.

Pourriyahi, Homa, Niloufar Yazdanpanah, et al. "Loneliness: An Immunometabolic Syndrome." *International Journal of Environmental Research and Public Health* 18, no. 22 (2021): 12162. https://doi.org/10.3390/ijerph182212162.

Qualben, Lars P. *A History of the Christian Church*. Wipf and Stock Publishers, 2008.

Rakel, David, et al. "Physician Empathy and Chronic Pain Outcomes." JAMA Network Open 6, no. 3 (2023): e235980. https://jamanetwork.com/journals/jamanetworkopen/fullarticle/2817441.

Sturgeon, John A. "Psychological Therapies for the Management of Chronic Pain." *Psychology Research and Behavior Management* 7 (2014): 115–24. https://doi.org/10.2147/PRBM.S44762.

Tedeschi, Richard G., and Lawrence G. Calhoun. "Posttraumatic Growth: Conceptual Foundations and Empirical Evidence." *Psychological Inquiry* 15, no. 1 (2004): 1–18. https://doi.org/10.1207/s15327965pli1501_01.

van der Kolk, Bessel. *The Body Keeps the Score: Brain, Mind, and Body in the Healing of Trauma*. Viking, 2014.

van Praag, H. M., E. R. de Kloet, and J. van Os. *Stress, the Brain and Depression.* Cambridge University Press, 2004.

Wang, Yanping, Bing Liu, Haojie Han, et al. "Associations Between Plant-Based Dietary Patterns and Risks of Type 2 Diabetes, Cardiovascular Disease, Cancer, and Mortality: A Systematic Review and Meta-Analysis." *Nutrition Journal* 22, no. 1 (2023): 46. https://doi.org/10.1186/s12937-023-00877-2.

Wright, N. T. *The Resurrection of the Son of God.* Fortress Press, 2003.

Yehuda, Rachel, and Amy Lehrner. "Intergenerational Transmission of Trauma Effects: Putative Role of Epigenetic Mechanisms." *World Psychiatry* 17, no. 3 (2018): 243–57. https://pmc.ncbi.nlm.nih.gov/articles/PMC6127768/.